COUNTER ATTACK FROM THE EAST

*Other Philosophical Works
by C. E. M. Joad*

George Allen & Unwin Ltd.
Philosophical Aspects of Modern Science
Essays in Commonsense Philosophy
New Edition

Oxford University Press
Matter, Life and Value
Introduction to Modern Political Theory
Introduction to Modern Philosophy

Methuen
Commonsense Ethics

Nisbet
Mind and Matter
etc.

COUNTER ATTACK FROM THE EAST

THE PHILOSOPHY OF RADHAKRISHNAN

by

C. E. M. JOAD

LONDON

GEORGE ALLEN & UNWIN LTD

MUSEUM STREET

FIRST PUBLISHED IN 1933

CONTENTS

NOTE

All books referred to without
the name of the author in
either text or footnotes are by
Radhakrishnan.

WEST AND EAST

CURRENT INDICTMENTS OF MODERN CIVILIZATION

That something is seriously amiss with the civilization of the West has been apparent for some time. The sense of dissatisfaction finds expression in a continuous series of books and articles; pulpits thunder denunciation on the frivolity of the age; economists and politicians warn us of impending collapse, while our great 'dailies' rumble with alarm as if they were the national bowels.

Our literature is clever and realistic, but it is uninspired; when it does acknowledge the draught of inspiration, it is so frankly animal that it would seem to blow from the stomach or the loins. Our social philosophy lacks definiteness of aim and purpose. We are apparently outgrowing democracy; certainly, it seems to serve our purposes with ever-diminishing success, yet our best minds shrink in dismay from the alternatives of Fascism and Communism, which are the only substitutes the age has as yet been able to evolve. Our art is decadent or sterile. Neither in music nor in painting has our age produced any figures comparable in stature with the great men of the past, and the flowing river of inspiration seems to have trickled away into the backwaters of formlessness, discord and experimentation for its own sake. Our poets write, not because they have something to say, but because it seems right to say something, and are so manifestly beating the air that Spengler boldly announces the approaching demise of art and advises young men to devote themselves "to technics rather than to lyrics."

Spengler, indeed, assuring us that our period of cultural growth is over and that there is nothing left for us but the stagnation of a rigid mechanical civilization, is our typical philosopher, at once the prop and mirror of the age, reflecting the tendencies which he has helped to form.

Our morals, if we are to believe the publicists, are shocking; young people, indulging their fancies and their instincts whenever they are pleased to feel them, do not hesitate to justify such indulgence in the name of self-expression and openly avow that the best way of getting rid of a temptation is to yield to it. Our conception of the good life is so debased that our rich men retiring from business can find no occupation for their leisure but striking little round pieces of matter with long thin ones in the shape of bats, mallets, cues, racquets and clubs, and introducing pieces of metal from a distance into the bodies of defenceless birds and animals; pursuits which prove so boring when adopted as staple occupations week in and week out, instead of as diversions for the week-end, that they return in dudgeon to their desks and continue to make money which they do not want in despair of finding life tolerable without the hard labour to

which they have been accustomed. And so on, and
so on. . . .

The indictment is a formidable one and ranges
over the whole field of contemporary life. Much of
it, no doubt, is beside the point; much may be
written off as an expression of the inevitable resent-
ment felt by elderly authors at the movement of
evolution for having passed them by; much again
could be and has been brought with equal justice
against any civilization in any age and is not specially
applicable to our own.

NATURE OF BOOK

But, when all allowance is made for these factors,
a formidable sense of dissatisfaction remains which
is not new but increasing. Something, I repeat, is
clearly amiss.

What? This book, in form an account of Radhakrishnan's philosophy, is in substance an attempt
to answer the question, for it is an answer to precisely
this question that Radhakrishnan's philosophy
purports to provide. Before I come to it, let me
try to bring a little more clearly into focus this
feeling of dissatisfaction which is so characteristic of
our civilization.

STATUS AND USES OF MODERN SCIENCE

The distinguishing achievement of the West is
science. Science has endowed Western man with
power over the forces of nature beyond the wildest
dreams of any previous civilization. It has unlocked

the secrets of the physical world; it has given man speed and dowered him with goods; it has shed light upon the dark places of his origin and past; it has charted the workings of his body and aspires not, without show of justification, to probe the mystery of his life. Unlike most of man's so-called knowledge it has practical uses. It has it in its power to rid the lives of human beings of dull and drudging work and their minds of superstitious fears. It has eased the grim burden of man's pain, and, what is scarcely less important, removed the overshadowing fear of pain. In a hundred ways it has brightened and cleansed human existence, and because of it the Western world is to-day a franker, a saner and in some ways a happier place than it has ever been in the past.

CONTRASTED WITH MODERN WISDOM

Unfortunately, however, man's wisdom has not developed commensurately with his powers. Science, as Bertrand Russell has pointed out, does not change man's desires; it merely increases his power of satisfying them. If the desires are good, this added power of satisfaction is itself a good; if evil, it is proportionately an evil. Now while human desires individually are neither good nor evil but mixed, owing to the fact that we still live in a state of international brigandage, they are in their social and collective expression mainly harmful. For this reason science, which has endowed civilized man with such prodigious powers, has endowed him to his peril; so much so, that he is within measurable distance of exterminating himself in the next war and mechanizing himself into a mere unit of production, if he avoids extermination. Hence, it is not enough for civilized man to be no worse than he ever was, if he is to avoid shipwreck; he has a need to be very much better, since, unless he can control the forces which science has unloosed, they will assuredly destroy him.

In obtaining such control the scientists themselves, with occasional rare exceptions,[1] show no disposition to participate. With impressive unanimity they disclaim responsibility for the uses to which society puts their results. Laboriously they explain that science is ethically and socially neutral; they are laboratory workers whose business it is to discover the operations of nature; what citizens choose to do with their discoveries is not their concern. It does not seem to occur to them that they too are citizens, and that it is their duty either to take a hand in administering the fruits of their work or to withhold their results until society shows itself fit to be entrusted with them. At the moment they are like men presenting babies with boxes of matches and schoolboys with high explosives without troubling to enquire whether the babies are likely to set fire to themselves with the probable result of consuming the scientists in the conflagration, or recognizing the

[1] A series of Leaders and Letters in *The New Statesman and Nation*, which have appeared since this Prologue was written, has extracted this qualification.

duty of instructing the schoolboys in the properties of T.N.T.

SCIENTISTS REFUSE TO TAKE A HAND

By this refusal of the scientists to assume social responsibilities society is deprived of the assistance of the brains of its most intelligent citizens, at a moment when it is more than usually embarrassed with their fruits. For this attitude of non-co-operation the scientist's traditional disinclination to come to conclusions without sufficient data is in part responsible. This disinclination, defensible and even necessary in the realms of physics and chemistry, argues a certain lack of realistic comprehension on the part of those who seek to extend it outside them. In spheres where the truth can be established it is right not to announce conclusions until they have been verified. But in philosophy, ethics and politics, no such verification is possible.

Yet human beings must live; they must also live in societies. Now living from its very nature involves the adoption of conclusions before they have been established; it also involves the need to act as if a certain course of conduct were right before one knows that it is right. In a word, to live is to take risks; so is to govern, to administer and to believe. Hence the attitude of strict agnosticism in the absence of necessary data which the scientist adopts in his own sphere is inappropriately extended beyond it. To insist that it must be so extended, to refuse, that is to say, to make up one's mind without adequate evidence in politics, ethics, theology, involves, indeed, in itself the adoption of a conclusion; for, as William James pointed out, to refuse to have faith merely because we have no conclusive evidence upon a particular issue, involves precisely the risk which it is sought to avoid. "Scepticism, then, is not avoidance of option. It is option of a certain particular kind of risk. *Better risk loss of truth than chance of error*—that is your faith vetoer's exact position. He is actively playing his stake as much as a believer is; he is backing the field against the religious hypothesis, just as the believer is backing the religious hypothesis against the field. . . . Dupery for dupery, what proof is there that dupery through hope is so much worse than dupery through fear?" So William James. . . . Nevertheless the Western world gets, and is likely to get, little help from the scientist when it approaches him for guidance in practical affairs. That his are the brains of our world most would agree; but in spite of his brains he seems incapable of telling us either what to believe or how to act. He can throw no light either upon the purpose of life as a whole or upon the immediate problems of how we are to live here and now.

IMPOTENCE OF PHILOSOPHY IN THE WEST

If he goes to the philosopher, the modern Westerner is in no better case. Philosophy began to be effective when Socrates asked the Athenians inconvenient questions in the market-place; it began, that is to say, with the interest which a man with an original mind took in the behaviour of his contemporaries and with his commentary upon and criticism of their behaviour. Throughout its history philosophy has alternated between maintaining this living contact with contemporary life and losing it; but the times when it has lost it have been the times when it has been least fruitful as philosophy. Our age must, assuredly, be reckoned one of these times. Philosophy, no doubt, must be different from life, but it should not be indifferent. Yet divorced from the flow of contemporary events philosophers make a merit of their aloofness, and, preoccupied with a barren controversy over episte-mology, devote themselves to the elaboration of a logical technique whose remoteness from practical issues gives point to the gibe that the problems of philosophy are less a substitute than an escape from those of life.

Recently there have been symptoms of a revival of interest in contemporary problems. Professor Whitehead's writings on religion, Bertrand Russell's excursions into sociology and politics, and Professor Macmurray's broadcast talks on problems of freedom and personality are symptoms of that interest. But the indifference of professional philosophers to these incursions by their contemporaries into the human field of hopes and wishes, problems and policies, is a measure of the depth of the academic shades by which their subject is shrouded.

TWILIGHT OF RELIGION

Our religion is one which many profess but few believe, and, the more educated, the fewer. A number of causes contribute to this result. In the first place, the spiritual truths of Christianity are presented in a context of dogmatic assertions in regard to scientific historical and geographical facts which observation and experiment have shown to be untrue. It is not true, for example, that the world was created in the way which our Scriptures assert, that the earth is immobile and the centre of the firmament, that there is a substance called the soul which leaves the body at death, that there is a geographical place called hell and another place called heaven, or that chemical substances such as bread and wine can be changed into substances of a different order by the use of certain forms of words.

The fact that these things are not so has no bearing upon the spiritual truth of the Christian religion; nevertheless, official Christianity as organized in the Churches insists on burdening itself with the lumber of its past, with the result that, when a choice is forced between the requirements of a faith based on authority on the one hand, and the facts of which his education supported by a plain reading of his personal experience has assured him on the other, the modern educated Westerner has little difficulty in making a decision. Inevitably, having made it, he is inclined to throw out the baby with the bath water, and to regard religion as

B

nonsense because he finds that the world was not
created in six days.

He is confirmed in this view by the manifest
incapacity of his Church to cope with the problems
of the time. In the recent war professed exponents
of the religion of Christ flatly contradicted every
principle of the teaching they were paid to profess.
Any attempt to draw attention to this teaching
was hushed into silence, and those who ventured
to act in accordance with it were imprisoned with
the ready concurrence of the Church. To-day the
Churches present the appearance of bodies too
preoccupied with professional disputations over
points of dogma and ritual to spare the time to
attend to the problems of contemporary life. When
they do intervene, their contribution is so patently
at variance with the spirit of Christ that the exas-
perated epigram, "For God's sake don't touch the
Church of England; it's the only thing that stands
between us and Christianity," which went the
unofficial rounds in the House of Commons at the
time of the debate on the Revised Prayer Book, is
not so wide of the mark as those who were ready to
be shocked by it supposed.

In general, the spirit of the West is markedly
hostile to religion in at least two senses of that
ambiguous word. It distrusts supernaturalism and
is sceptical of any transcendental account of the
nature of the universe; and it knows enough comparative religion to distrust the claim to exclusive
and exhaustive truth historically made by most of

the great religions and by none more eagerly than by its own Christianity. Nevertheless the Westerner badly needs a faith. Ill at ease in the spiritual vacuum left by the decay of traditional beliefs, he expresses his loneliness by a feverish clutching at any straw that seems likely to lend him support. The fact is that he dislikes facing the infinite single-handed as much as he dislikes facing the problem of conduct with nothing better than his own good sense to guide him.

THE CASE OF ETHICS

Guidance has traditionally been provided by codes of ethics; but ethics in the contemporary West is in no better case than religion. Inevitably, since it is to a large extent derivative from religion. The Christian religion has historically backed the contemporary code of morals, whatever the conduct which at any given moment it may have enjoined, by the promise of rewards and the threat of punishment, with the result that it is difficult to say how much of what has been accounted good behaviour in the past has been prompted by the desire to achieve an eternity of celestial bliss and to avoid an eternity of infernal torment. This, of course, is to turn ethics into a system of post-dated Hedonism —one eschews the more obvious pleasures now in order to make sure of enjoying more quintessential pleasures in perpetuity hereafter—nor do I wish to suggest that these purely prudential considerations have ever been the *sole* motive for right conduct.

The fact remains, however, that religion in the West has taken good care to present both the rewards and the punishments in the liveliest colours, so that the relaxation of ethical restraints which has accompanied the decay of religious belief need cause no surprise. The tendency has been reinforced by the reaction from the purely inhibitory morality of our Victorian ancestors, who never called a pleasure a pleasure when they could call it a sin, and by the object lesson of the war as a collective practical repudiation of all the ethical principles officially accepted by the West as forming the essential message of Christ.

In the absence of any code of conduct which it could accept the post-war generation adopted the gospel of self-expression. This, whatever it may mean for a mature sage, found its chief application in a contemptuous repudiation of all the preferences and prejudices which the Victorians pretentiously called their morals as a preliminary to the adoption of a frankly avowed Hedonism.

The defect of Hedonism as a rule of life is that, if you persistently make pleasure your aim, you find after a short experience that nothing pleases. Unfortunately this is a truth which nobody accepts until he has discovered it for himself, with the result that the phase of post-war licence has been succeeded by a post-post-war phase of disillusionment. Two aspects of this phase may be noted.

NEED FOR A CREED AND A CODE

(i) First, as regards conduct, ordinary men and women find themselves for the first time in modern civilization without any accepted code of right and wrong. The lack would not seriously embarrass the original moral genius or the constitutional moral rebel. The ordinary man, however, being neither a moral genius nor a moral rebel, is accustomed to get his code of beliefs and morals as he gets his clothes and his boots ready made from the social shop, believing in Allah and polygamy, if he happens to be born in a palace in Constantinople, as readily as he believes in the Trinity and monogamy, if he is born in a bedroom in Balham. In practice his moral needs are limited to a demand for rules of conduct which he can understand and respect, and, provided that these are definite and generally recognized, their precise content is comparatively unimportant. "Tell me what to think and what to do" is the cry of the ordinary man all through the ages, and, because they have told him, the Church and the Army have always been his two most popular institutions. To deprive such a one of the guidance to which he has been accustomed, is to lay him under the necessity of making his rules for himself and deciding each issue on merits, as an alternative to moral anarchy. Lacking the equipment for the first and the taste for the second, he is in a state of bewildered agnosticism. Endowed with a constitutional craving for authority and guidance, he is yet disabled by the scepticism of his age from accepting any of the numerous claimants for the favour of his credulity in the field.

LACK OF SENSE OF VALUES

(ii) In the second place, he acknowledges no scale of values. That Western civilization is deplorably lacking in a sense of value is implicit in all that I have said of the marvels of our science and of the use to which we put them. Modern Western civilization is the result of endowing with the fruits of the work of a dozen men of genius a population which is emotionally at the level of savages and culturally at that of schoolboys. In this disparity between our mechanical expertness and our social and ethical lack of it lies, I have suggested, the great danger to our civilization. There was never more leisure at man's disposal for the living of the good life; there was never less knowledge of how to live it. See that mechanic mending the carburettor of his car. In his knowledge of material forces and skill in its application he is behaving rather like a superman. See the same mechanic ten minutes later driving in a little hell of noise and dust and stench, unable to appreciate the country himself and precluding the appreciation of all who come near him; he is behaving like a congenital idiot! Men of genius by the dozen, men of talent by the hundred, have laboured that wireless might be; they succeeded, and the tittle-tattle of the green-room and the racing stable is broadcast to the furthest Pacific, while the remoter ether vibrates to the strains of negroid music.

ILLUSTRATION FROM THE 'TALKIES'

Of all the expressions of Western civilization the 'talkies' are the most striking and the most characteristic. Their production involves a miracle of applied science. The essential constituent involved in the production of a 'talkie' is a photo-electric cell. When light of short wavelength falls upon a clean metal surface, it is found that the surface becomes charged with positive electricity. This positive charge is due to the emission from the surface of electrons, little particles of negative electricity, which are jerked out of it by the short wavelength rays. If the inside of an evacuated glass bulb is coated with a suitable metal so as to provide an interior metal surface, and a wire be inserted into the bulb which conducts the electrons away as they are jerked out, a small electric current passes along the wire. This current varies with the strength of the light rays falling on the bulb. The bulb so prepared is known as a photo-electric cell. By the aid of this apparatus fluctuations in light are transformed into fluctuations of electric current. These in their turn can be transformed into fluctuations of sound. Now fluctuations of sound can be made to produce fluctuations of light by the use of very thin plates of metal which respond to sound. By means of these fluctuating thin plates a band of light and dark alternations which correspond to the sounds of speech or music is printed on the side of a film. The intervals between the light and dark portions of the band represent the characteristics of and relations between different sounds. When it is desired to reproduce the original sounds, the band is run in the path of a beam of light. The beam of light then fluctuates in a manner corresponding to the sounds which produced the band. This beam in its turn is made to fall on a photo-electric cell and so to produce a fluctuating current of liberated electrons which can be translated back again into sound.

To have discovered these processes and to have perfected a device to give effect to the discovery is surely among the marvels of the human intellect. And this incredible apparatus is devoted to the representation of a series of dramas in which the warfare of battling stags for the favour of does is regarded as the only legitimate object of human interest, played by elaborately under-dressed women who titillate our senses while they debauch our taste, and men whose carefully ironed features and swelling muscles suggest that brawn has finally and completely triumphed over brain.

REPUDIATION OF OBJECTIVE VALUE

Nor is there any sign of revolt from the scale of values, or rather, of disvalues, that our most popular form of entertainment implies. On the contrary, that there are neither values nor disvalues, but only personal preferences and prejudices is one of the most cherished convictions of the contemporary young. There are, they insist, no great men and women; there are only those whom individual historians have delighted to praise. There are no great artists and musicians; there are only those who happen to appeal to the taste of a particular generation. As I write, there comes into my mind the picture of a student attached to a pair of earphones by means of which he was listening to wireless jazz, while he was at the same time reading Hegel; and to the questions did not the one activity interfere with the other, and was it in any event advisable to mix the trivial with the noble, the froth of the day with the great thoughts of all time, replying that to say of one activity or form of enjoyment that it is *better* than another is meaningless. All that one is entitled to assert, he declared, is that it is more or less satisfying to the mood of the moment. The remark was characteristic—characteristic of a refusal to discriminate which arises from a fundamental scepticism as to the reality of those values which have been traditionally regarded as the ends of human action.

Scepticism in matters of belief, guidelessness in matters of conduct, indifference in regard to value, these are the outstanding factors in the mood of the West. The result is that nowhere in the Western world to-day is there any accepted view as to what men ought to believe, how they ought to act, or what things they ought to admire. The situation is admirably brought out in the play of Shaw's old age, *Too True to be Good*.

"TOO TRUE TO BE GOOD"

Shaw began his propagandist career forty years ago by urging the world to win free from the swathes and swaddling of Victorian sentimentality and romanticism, to learn self-knowledge, to confront itself. He succeeded, only to find that the process of stripping Western man of his illusions has left him as uncomfortable as stripping him of his clothes. Now that the blinkers are off and Western man sees, or thinks he sees, things as they are, he is confronted with a vision of himself straying naked and forlorn through an indifferent universe, a mere target for the shafts of doom, twitched into love and war, creeds and causes by a showman who, indifferent alike to his weal and woe, pulls the strings. Lacking creed, faith and purpose, he cannot endure the emptiness of his own soul, cannot be pleased by pleasures that he sees through, cannot be comforted by loyalties and ideals once absolute but riddled now with his scepticism. The characters in this latest play, the embittered atheist, the disillusioned clergyman, the disgruntled airman, the girl 'Mops' who throws convention to the winds that she may have 'a good time,' and being free, healthy and happy, is yet dissatisfied and miserable, are each and all asking in different accents the same question: What way of life shall I pursue that I may escape the dreadful humiliation of the nakedness of my soul? This question is the theme of the speech of inspired eloquence with which the play ends.

"It is clear to me that though they are dispersing quietly to do very ordinary things . . . yet they are all falling, falling, falling, endlessly and hopelessly through a void in which they can find no footing. There is something fantastic about them, something unreal and perverse, something profoundly unsatisfactory. . . . Naked bodies no longer shock us, but the horror of the naked mind is still more than we can bear.

"Swear; use dirty words; drink cocktails; kiss and caress and cuddle, until girls who are like roses at eighteen are like battered demireps at twenty-two; in all these ways the bright young things of the victory have scandalized their pre-war elders, and left nobody but their bright young selves a penny the worse. But how are we to bear this dreadful new nakedness? The iron lightning of war has burnt great rents in our angelic veils of idealism, just as it has smashed great holes in our cathedral roofs and torn great gashes in our hillsides. Our souls go in rags now.

"I stand mid-way between youth and age, like a man who has missed his train: too late for the last one and too early for the next. . . . I have no Bible, no creed: the war has shot both out of my hands. . . . I am ignorant: I have lost my nerve and am intimidated; all I know is that I must find the way of life for myself and all of us, or we shall surely perish. . . ."

WHAT SHALL I DO TO BE SAVED?

The question is implied in what in America is called, at the time of writing, "the depression," which is a condition of mind even more than a condition of markets. It is implicit in the armed fear of Europe and in the defeatism which lies like a black cloud over the Western world. It expresses the fundamental need of contemporary civilization, a shorn lamb to whom God has not yet tempered the wind of truth. It is the cry of children who, having outgrown their old toys, have not yet learnt the use of new ones. The Western world, indeed, is passing through a period common enough in precocious children, in which knowledge is greater than the wisdom which should assimilate it. We are in consequence both arrogant and frightened; arrogant, when we look without and parade our achievements before the East; frightened, when we look within and gauge their effects upon ourselves. To sum up, in the words of the peasant apprised of the marvels of the age, quoted in Radhakrishnan's *Kalki*:— "We are taught to fly in the air like birds, and to swim in the water like fishes; but how to live on the earth we do not know."[1] The remark in its way is epic; it epitomizes the commentary of one civilization upon another, conveying the reaction of the traditional philosophy of the East to the contemporary achievement of the West.

[1] *Kalki*, p. 9.

CIVILIZATIONS OF THE EAST

In the East is a civilization which, whatever its other defects, has escaped the distinguishing faults of the West. It does not identify the good life with the transfer of pieces of matter from one place to another; it takes no mystic delight in the impact of oblong pieces of matter upon round ones; and it does not regard rapid motion upon the earth's surface in mechanisms propelled by petrol as the most praiseworthy human activity. It values machines, in so far as it puts up with them at all, not as ends in themselves but as means to ends beyond themselves, the lightening of human toil and the increase of human leisure. Also its members know how to employ leisure. Unlike most Westerners, they can sit still and listen; they can bear themselves by themselves, and many possess the technique of solitude and are trained in the art of meditation. The civilizations of the East are very old; their roots stretch far back into the past to a time when Europe was still a cockpit of fighting savages. "Long before Western Europe had emerged from the Stone Age, the civilizations of Egypt, Babylon, Assyria, Crete and Chaldea had reached a highly advanced stage. If we confine our attention to the last 6,000 years of our history and represent one hundred years by a minute of the clock . . . we find that Egypt and Babylon are holding the centre of the stage when the hands are at twelve . . . China, India and Media come upon the scene at twenty past twelve. . . .

At twelve forty-five we are in the beginnings of the powerful, modern European nations. Every minute of the next ten an Empire or a kingdom goes off the map and another comes on. A few seconds before one o'clock we had the Great War."[1] In short, if we reckon the span of human civilization at about five thousand years, India has been civilized more or less throughout the whole of that period, Europe during only one-sixth of it.

Now during this protracted period of five thousand years of civilization certain traditions of living have been built up. These traditions are bound up with the cultivation of certain spiritual values. Because of their preoccupation with these values, the life of action and ambition has never had quite the same hold upon men in the East as it has in the West. What do I mean by 'spiritual values'?

THEIR LONGEVITY

The question formulates itself inevitably in the Westerner's mind, apt at all times to be distrustful of what it regards as the 'woolliness' of the thought which is normally expressed in such phrases, and, after the admitted fiasco of religion in the last war, a fiasco brought about by a disparity between practice and profession so flagrant that even the Church could not avoid being struck by it, particularly distrustful of spiritual 'woolliness.' The question is one which it is Radhakrishnan's main business to answer, and, if I am successful in con-

[1] *Kalki*, pp. 49, 50.

veying the gist of his religious philosophy, by the time I have finished my readers will be able to answer it for themselves. Meanwhile, it is worth while noting that the life of the spirit, whatever one means by it, appears to confer a certain longevity upon nations who practise it. It is the energetic active peoples who are for ever going about their worldly business who are short lived. Overmuch taking thought for the morrow is apt to preclude one from being present on the morrow when it comes.

If we survey the rise and fall of civilizations in the past, we see that those which devoted their energies to politics, patriotism and aggrandizement, have either destroyed themselves by their own restlessness from within or have made themselves so intolerable to their neighbours that they have been forced to destroy them from without.

REBUKE FROM THE EAST

At the moment the Western world is within measurable distance of destroying itself through its inability to control the forces with which its science has endowed it. The next European war is likely to see the end of European civilization, while the social incidence of the unchecked powers of production is in a fair way to bring about a collapse of an economic system which seems incapable of distributing what it produces. Our nations too, no less than our individuals, might do well to take a leaf out of the book of the East and, instead of perpetually 'doing,' learn to sit back and listen.

In short, while the East knows little of machines, while the material apparatus of its civilization is of the crudest and its residents fail to move either rapidly or frequently over and above the surface of the earth, it inherits from its long line of seers and sages a traditional wisdom in the light of which men may live at peace and be content. It is by virtue of the insight of this traditional wisdom that the West stands rebuked: "A community which is almost entirely occupied with life and body, physical and economic existence, scientific and technical efficiency to the exclusion of the higher humanistic ideals of mind and spirit is not truly civilized."[1] Can the wisdom be communicated, so that we may be moved to rebuke ourselves?

It is precisely here that Radhakrishnan, whom you have just heard speaking in the wings, enters to make his bow; or rather, for I must keep him and you waiting a moment longer, here is the entrance through which, in these pages, he will most frequently take the stage. There is, however, another through which he will make his appearance, not so often, but none the less effectively.

DECADENCE OF THE EAST

In writing of the East as the guardian of a traditional way of life which the West has lost, the repository of certain values which the West has forgotten or never known, I have given only one side of the picture. To complete it I must add that

[1] *Kalki*, p. 42.

the guardian is tottering on the verge of senility, and the repository is less like a safe than a worm-eaten trunk liable to fall to pieces at any moment through lack of repairs. "But Hinduism lives so little. Listlessness reigns now where life was once like a bubbling spring. We are to-day drifting, not advancing, waiting for the future to turn up. There is a lack of vitality, a spiritual flagging. Owing to our political vicissitudes, we ignored the law of growth. In the great days of Hindu civilization it was quick with life, crossing the seas, planting colonies, teaching the world as well as learning from it. In sciences and arts, in trade and commerce it was not behind the most advanced nations of the world till the middle of this millennium. To-day we seem to be afraid of ourselves, and are therefore clinging to the shell of our religion for self-preservation. The envelope by which we try to protect life checks its expansion."[1]

In this time-worn corpus of knowledge—or should it be tradition?—there are at last signs of change. "After a long winter of some centuries, we are to-day in one of the creative periods of Hinduism. We are beginning to look upon our ancient faith with fresh eyes. We feel that our society is in a condition of unstable equilibrium."[2] The change envisaged is said to be not a surrender of the principles of Hinduism, a faltering in allegiance to the values of which I have spoken, "but a restatement of them with special reference to the needs of a

[1] *The Hindu View of Life*, p. 128.   [2] Ibid., p. 130.

more complex and mobile social order."[1] It is a change which involves the reaffirmation of their validity in a new setting. So Radhakrishnan on the present state of the culture he is about to expound.

It is time to summarize the foregoing. The West has the energy and vitality of a civilization still comparatively young, yet does not know into what channels to direct them. Possessing in abundance the means to the good life, it is without knowledge of the end. The East possesses the tradition and the knowledge, but is without the vitality to make the tradition live or the knowledge spread, and is in danger of being swamped by the vigorous tides that flow from the West. Each lacks something that is essential, each has something to give. Can they, then, be brought together?

[1] *The Hindu View of Life*, p. 130.

COUNTER ATTACK
FROM THE EAST

CHAPTER I

RADHAKRISHNAN THE *LIAISON* OFFICER

I. Impact upon the West

THE LECTURER

And now at last Radhakrishnan, who has been waiting somewhat impatiently, I am afraid—for he is not as patient as his rôle of Eastern sage demands—in the wings, may come forward and make his bow.

It is an arresting personality who takes his call —a spare slight figure, a keen alert face, and a pair of bright brown eyes. All these you will notice, but notice only to forget at the sound of the beautifully modulated voice conveying in a series of exquisitely turned phrases an equal mastery of the intricacies of the English language and of Hindu metaphysics. Much has been written of Radhakrishnan the thinker, but of Radhakrishnan the talker and listener not enough. For his performances in this line are startling. He has so mastered the technique of lecturing as to turn what as practised by most of us is an effort of sweating exegesis, as painful for lecturer as for lecturees, into the apparently effortless performance of an art. He is extremely fluent and his lectures, delivered entirely without notes, flow in a stream of perfectly turned sentences which would put most English speakers to shame. One expects a Hindu to be eloquent, and Radhakrishnan is on occasions very eloquent. But for wit one is less prepared. Yet it is as a wit rather than as an orator that he has chiefly impressed himself upon the present writer, possibly, perhaps, because wit is a fruit which grows so rarely in the lush jungle of Hindu thought. I do not mean that he is deliberately witty; his frequent epigrams result less from a forced collocation of ideas than from the drive of his thought seeking its logical and most appropriate expression. "It takes centuries of life to make a little history; it takes centuries of history to produce a little tradition"; the millennium "is a time when all the heads will be hard and all the pillows soft!" His lectures are punctuated with such remarks and they will be found continually in his books. Withal his style is pleasant and easy, enriched with simile and metaphor, and illuminated with vivid and arresting phrases. It crystallizes regularly and naturally into these phrases: "To be ignorant is not the special prerogative of man; to know that he is ignorant is his special privilege." "Balfour defended 'philosophic doubt' only to establish the foundations of belief." I have taken these quotations at random from consecutive pages of his recently published Hibbert Lectures, and they could be paralleled from almost any page in the book.

HIS ATTRACTION FOR THE WESTERNER

I have attended a number of Radhakrishnan's lectures and they were always crowded to the doors. The Hibbert Lectures, delivered at University College, constituted an event even in the crowded life of London. The audience was notable not only because of its size but because of its quality. Most of those attending were young! The lectures formed no part of a recognized University Course and attendance was, therefore, optional. Nevertheless, young men and women, many of whom, to my knowledge, had been earning their living as clerks, teachers, salesmen and typists since half-past nine in the morning, while others had, I suppose, already attended a couple of lectures on the same day, were there in hundreds, listening to a profoundly religious man expounding to a generation which has largely lost its religion, a profoundly religious view of life.

The West—we are not allowed to forget the fact— has lost its religion, yet misses what it has lost; its attitude is that of a wistful agnosticism. Radhakrishnan comes from a country in which religion is known to be still a living force; therefore, argued the audience, he may have something to offer which may be of use to us. What that 'something' is, it will be the business of this book to try to make plain. Meanwhile, let us in passing recognize Radhakrishnan as the heir to a great tradition. Wise men before now have come from the East, and they have rarely come empty handed. He almost certainly has something up his spiritual sleeve to which we will be well advised to pay heed.

THE BRIDGE BUILDER

But, if Radhakrishnan brings something from the East to offer to the West, the debt is not wholly one-sided. As was hinted in the last chapter, all is not well with religion, even in the East. The religion of the Hindus is static; it lacks vitality; it seems at times to be a tired religion. To it Radhakrishnan offers the vitalizing energy and the restless curiosity of the West. 'Do not,' he seems to say to his fellow-countrymen, 'imagine that you are the repositories of all wisdom merely because you are the vehicle of a wise tradition. It is your business to enrich that tradition. Evolution is a fact; the world changes; spirit grows and develops. The truths of yesterday are often only the half-truths of to-day. Do not think you possess the whole of the stick merely because you hold the right end of it.'

And so the function, the unique function, which Radhakrishnan fulfils to-day is that of a *liaison* officer. He seeks to build a bridge between the traditional wisdom of the East and the new knowledge and energy of the West, that each may be enriched by the qualities of the other. Synthesis and reconstruction are his objectives, and he believes that they can be most effectively achieved by a revival of religion. "Religious idealism," he says, "seems to be the most hopeful political instrument for peace which the world has seen. . . . Treaties and diplomatic understandings may restrain passions, but they do not remove fear. The world must be imbued with a love of humanity. We want religious heroes who will not wait for the transformation of the whole world, but assert with their lives if necessary the truth of the conviction 'on earth one family'."[1]

EFFECT UPON A EUROPEAN MIND

For the post of *liaison* officer between two civilizations Radhakrishnan possesses a rare combination of qualities. To the European he seems to be himself at times a child of the West. It may be merely the effect of his quality of intellectual sympathy which enables him to open his mind so completely to the man to whom he is talking that one feels an immediate and instinctive kinship; but it is a fact that with him I have felt almost for the first time in such intercourse as I have had with Indians, "This man is at bottom the same sort of animal as I am. He feels broadly what I feel; thinks as I think." With him for the first time in talking to a man from the East, I have been conscious of that jolly march of mind with mind, which is the condition of all comfortable and fruitful intellectual intercourse.

I do not mean merely that Radhakrishnan is steeped in the waters of modern thought and has European philosophy so completely at his fingerends that inevitably one has topics in common;

[1] *Kalki*, p. 96.

I mean also that his method of approach to a subject, his habit of discussion and argument, his capacity for seeing a point when it is made and then either answering or conceding it, seem to the Western mind fundamentally akin to its own. His mind has a definiteness, a precision, which, if I may venture the remark without offence, is all too rare a characteristic in the modern Hindu. He knows the virtues of order and arrangement and is a clear and capable expositor. Important qualities these in a man who offers to guide you through the jungle of Hindu thought. He does not, except when he is very excited, mistake rhetoric for argument, or believe that the mere process of asserting something in a number of different and increasingly eloquent ways somehow makes it true. I do not want to assert that Indian thinkers do these things, but they certainly sometimes give to Englishmen the impression that they do. And he does not make the mistake of crediting his Western hearers with a knowledge of Indian philosophy and religion, and save himself the trouble of difficult and perhaps inevitably misleading translation into English by the lazy assumption that they will understand Indian technical terms such as guru, mukti, dharma, or even Karma. It is a fact that the average Westerner does not know what these terms mean; it is also a fact that most Indians seem quite unable to realize. The point seems a small one, but its neglect is a source of endless exasperation, and Radhakrishnan's failure to neglect it is a good example of that imaginative intellectual sympathy of which I have already spoken.

PERSONAL TRAITS

Withal Radhakrishnan remains in all essentials the Hindu sage. As such he gives the impression of one who knows his own way in life so well that no possible combination of circumstances could make him turn aside from his chosen path. I do not mean that he is a dogmatist, although I imagine his fundamental convictions are not liable to be easily shaken; merely that he has an attitude—an attitude which is the inheritance of centuries of tradition—to the practical problems of life, the problem of the government of oneself, the problem of self-expression and self-devotion to others, the problem of desire and the restraint of desire, which he maintains with unvarying consistency. This attitude gives him poise and dignity, and an ease of bearing adequate to all the various occasions of social intercourse. It makes his vegetarianism and teetotalism seem not, as they so frequently do in Europeans, mere whims and affectations, or the fruit of the cold-blooded and rather defiant application of *a priori* principles, but the inevitable and appropriate expression of a deliberately adopted way of life, which is applied in practice with as little fuss as most of us evince in blowing our noses or raising our hats to a lady in the street.

It enables him to talk with ease and opportunity to all sorts and conditions of men—Radhakrishnan can on occasions be one of the most stimulating conversationalists I know—and, what perhaps is a greater achievement, to be silent with all sorts and conditions of men; silent, that is, not with the silence of the fool who has nothing to say but just enough sense to know it, but with the significance of one who has deliberately chosen to listen, that he may the better enrich the stores of his experience and increase his understanding of the thoughts and ways of men.

A DINNER PARTY

I shall not easily forget dining in company with Radhakrishnan at H. G. Wells's flat. Besides Wells and myself there was only one other person present, J. W. N. Sullivan, the well-known writer on scientific subjects. The talk was continuous and eager; it included science, philosophy, the state of the world, the possible collapse of Western civilization. Radhakrishnan was for the most part silent. He sat there refusing one after another the dishes of an elaborate meal, drinking only water, listening. We others, knowing his reputation as a speaker and a conversationalist were, I think, a little surprised at this silence; surprised, and impressed, not so much because what he did say was always to the point, but because his silence in such a discussion was a richer and more significant thing than any positive contribution he could have made. It was the silence of a completely integrated personality, deliberately absorbing an atmosphere. To suggest an idea to the ordinary man is like dropping a stone into a deep well. One hears the splash of the impact, and then silence. What happens thereafter is unknown; so far as any evidence to the contrary goes, the idea has been completely buried in the bowels of the personality. Certainly it never re-emerges. To talk to Radhakrishnan is not like that. The idea sinks in but only to re-emerge, reclothed and trans-figured by the alchemy of a very subtle mind. Assuredly a fruitful and significant experience! I was not surprised at the warmth of Wells's leave-taking despite the silence of the guest.

Such, in general, is the effect of Radhakrishnan upon a typical Western mentality. He is, one notices at once, at his ease; he has assurance; he steers effortlessly an even course between the Scylla of self-assertion and the Charybdis of undue humility; yet never for a moment does he cease to be a Hindu. In sum, his personality is no less calculated to intrigue the curiosity of the Western world than his wisdom is, as I hope to show, fitted to compose its distraction.

II. Influence upon the East

RADHAKRISHNAN AND THE NEW HINDUISM

It is obvious that a chapter which presents Radhakrishnan in the light of a *liaison* officer between East and West should introduce him not only from the English but from the Indian end. How is Radhakrishnan regarded in contemporary

India? What is his specific contribution to its thought? What is his attitude to its problems? What his effect upon his countrymen? These questions, it is obvious, should be answered if the account is to be complete. Yet this undoubtedly necessary work of completion offers to the present author great difficulty. I have not visited India. I am almost completely ignorant of its problems and have comparatively little knowledge of its literature and philosophy.

But, as Radhakrishnan has been the subject of many eulogies and some criticism by contemporary Indian writers, there is a fair amount of literature dealing with the man and his views, some of which I have consulted.

Radhakrishnan has identified himself with the movement known as the "New Hinduism," which, while maintaining, seeks to revitalize the old Hindu culture. In recent years he has delivered a series of Convocation addresses at different Universities, in all of which the same note is sounded. Indians are exhorted to shake off the oppressive traditions of the past and equip themselves to face the future, a future in which they will be called upon to play their part as leaders, statesmen and administrators in the national life of a self-governing India. Hindu life and thought are still, so runs the argument of the addresses, oppressed by traditionalism; upon Indian institutions there lies heavy the dead hand of the past. Against this influence progressive Indians are in revolt. They are in revolt not only against the continued domination of Indians by the British, but against their continued domination by their own past.

A brief summary of some of the main points from Radhakrishnan's University addresses will exhibit him in the rôle of spokesman of this revolt. I select for the purpose his Convocation addresses delivered to the Universities of Mysore and Lucknow in October 1930 and December 1931 respectively.

THE FUNCTION OF CULTURE

The business of a university is, he begins by pointing out, to give understanding and to transmit culture. Culture does not consist in the acquisition of shop-window goods whose price can be quoted, whose value assessed in terms of immediate advantage. Hence it is difficult to define, and, to an age increasingly governed by the stomach and pocket view of life, difficult to defend. Culture may, however, best be symbolized by "a torch that is passed on from hand to hand down the generations." But a lighted torch is a dangerous gift since it is the spirit of enquiry that kindles it; of enquiry and dissatisfaction with that which enquiry reveals. "It has stirred many an upheaval, started many a conflagration. It symbolizes the spirit of revolution; the cleansing fire which burns the wood, hay and stubble that have come down to us. If we are afraid of the upturnings of the soil, of the social, economic and political upheavals consequent on the spread of this fire, we should not go near a

University." The English reader thinks, or tries to, of the revolutionary fires that blaze at Oxford or Cambridge, and failing, concludes that Universities in India must be much more exciting and dangerous places than in England. They are not; but Radhakrishnan would have them so.

THE BUSINESS OF A UNIVERSITY

What a University must do is to "foster the type of mind that does not take the usual for granted, that makes conventions fluid, that does not believe that its ways of thought and life are a part of the eternal order of nature. . . . If it takes hold of the young with all the fullness and ardour of their youth and turns them into timid, selfish and conservative men, if it petrifies their ideas and freezes their initiative, the University has failed as a University."

Judged by this test Indian Universities are failures. Speaking of contemporary students Radhakrishnan censures the modern mind for the formation of which the Universities are presumably in part responsible, as being "singularly servile to its teachers and leaders. It will believe almost anything it is told. It is intellectually timid, and prefers to take its opinions from others."

CRITICISM OF INDIAN SPIRITUALITY

The criticism of the student is developed into an indictment of a nation. Radhakrishnan has no patience with a system which condemns millions of people to grinding poverty and blasting disease,

while preening itself on the score of spirituality for
its superiority to purely material considerations.
"We hear on all sides of the revolt of youth. . . .
My complaint is that it is not sufficiently widespread.
The general tendency to regard our ancient civilization as idealistic and the modern one as materialistic
is not the expression of revolt but of reaction. . . .
There is nothing idealistic about disease or poverty,
nothing spiritual in a system that uses human
beings as beasts of burden."

Indian spirituality, he implies, is too often a
mere rationalization of a lazy indifferentism, which
refuses to notice the sores in the body politic in
order the better to disclaim responsibility for that
for which it is collectively accountable; a criticism
this which might have come straight out of Fabian
Essays, so unmistakably is it inspired by the socialist
spirit of the modern West. It follows that a change
of mind is required as a condition of a change
in society. To his audience of Hindu students
Radhakrishnan denounces "our lack of ordinary
interest in communities other than our own, our
unthinking adoption of practices and prohibitions,
our social tyranny which makes cowards or automata
of most of us, our religious fanaticism. . . ." Hence
the call to young men to "revolt against a corrupt
social order and religious fanaticism." The future,
they are assured, is with them, not merely in the
ordinary rhetorical sense of the phrase in which
the speaker assures his audience that the future is
'with' whatever he happens to be advocating at

the moment, with the object of convincing them that he and they are on the winning side, but in the very special sense in which young Indians must look forward to a day when for the first time for centuries they will assume responsibility for the government of their own country.

CHALLENGE TO INDIAN YOUTH

There is, indeed, a special need for the training, for the dedication even, of Indian youth, since it is the behaviour of the coming generation which will decide the issue between a free yet ordered community growing to self-conscious nationhood, and the anarchy of national disruption. Many contemporary Indians appear to think that the mere withdrawal of the British will inaugurate the millennium. Radhakrishnan has no patience with this view: "We cannot make a Utopia to order. The first essential for achieving political freedom, as well as for guarding it when attained, is a juster social order." It is idle to expect the mere withdrawal of the British to usher in the millennium; "we must build a social structure rooted in principles of truth, freedom and equality."

The challenge to Indian youth to reconstruct the social and economic order of their country is, it is obvious, based on the assumption that the British will leave India, and that upon Indians will accordingly devolve the responsibility of self-government. Can this assumption be justified? Radhakrishnan thinks that it can. On the subject of the British in

India his views are clear cut and, I should imagine, fairly representative of the progressive Indian mind.

THE BRITISH IN INDIA

The principles of freedom and self-government originated in England. From there they have spread in theory and the abstract all over the world, reaching, still in theory and the abstract, India. Their influence on India was for long and might still have remained academic, were it nor for the continuous stream of Indians which for the last fifty years has flowed into the English Universities, where young Hindus have imbibed the ideas of John Stuart Mill, Bernard Shaw and Bertrand Russell. It was not in the nature of things to be expected that they should fail to apply the lessons they had learnt to the situation of their own country. "It is," says Radhakrishnan, "the study of Western history and institutions" which "has roused in us a love of freedom and a sense of self-respect." "I do not believe that there is a single Britisher who is loyal to his own history and true to his own tradition who will deny the legitimacy of India's claim to Indian rule." But while in England professors have lauded to Indian students the claims of theoretical freedom, in India our administrators have denied the practice of the theory our thinkers combine to commend. Thus England herself is doubly responsible for Indian unrest. If the policy of our rulers has provoked the demand for freedom, it is the teaching of our great men that has implanted the love of it.

D

What should be the outcome of the present situation? Radhakrishnan advocates the solution of Dominion Home Rule. He looks for a settlement by which "India is content to remain a member of the British Empire without sacrifice of her pride, self-respect and freedom of independent nationhood. . . . India will not refuse to remain a member of the British Empire, if such membership means connection with Great Britain for mutual advantage, and not control by Great Britain for her own interests."

THE TRUE BASIS OF ASSOCIATION

The ideal which, it is clear, he has in mind is that of an association between equals for mutual advantage, an association in which Englishmen and Indians, standing at the confluence of their respective streams of human culture, should blend the two, and, enriched by the blend, carry the human spirit to heights hitherto unrealized. Each has something to give which the other lacks; each is limited by the lack of that which the other has to give. A pooling of talents and cultures should pave the way for the evolution of a type of human being more developed in point of mental accomplishment and spiritual endowment than the world has yet seen. Nor is the interchange of material goods for mutual economic advantage overlooked. Such an "association may be the outer expression of the ultimate synthesis between the East and West." It may also be the nucleus "of a smaller League of Nations" working within the world polity for international peace.

But—again and again Radhakrishnan returns to the point—such an association must be based on equality and respect. The basis of the present association in the assumed racial superiority of one people to another must go; the basis is as unsound as the assumption is insulting. It is because "smaller minds interpret the British connection in a sordid way"; it is because Empire has meant in the past, and still, for many, means in the present, "markets for the central power, men, money and munitions for planting the flag in the extremes of the world . . . the massing of troops in a variety of colours against similar groupings on battle fronts . . . the exploitation of the weak and the backward," that forward-looking Hindus denounce the British connection and desire to cut loose from it. It is because Empire so conceived is "a vulgarity, a reaction, a danger to the peace of the world," that there is dissatisfaction in India to-day.

THE CALL TO INDIA

But in the last resort it is not the British connection which chiefly arouses Radhakrishnan's apprehension, because, perhaps, in the last resort he does not wish that India should disown it; it is the conservatism of his own countrymen. No man has stressed more urgently than Radhakrishnan the apathy and backwardness of India; no man is more alive than he to the elements in the national life that make it difficult for India to cope with her own problems.

And so we find him again and again inveighing against the excessive traditionalism, the exaggerated respect for the past, the indifference to human health and happiness, the racial feuds and religious factions which prevent India from growing to nationhood. It is this unfitness for government that produces the sense of urgency, of imminent crisis which can be felt in his appeals to young men. He is so deeply imbued with the sense that there is no time to lose.

It is this same sense of urgency which makes the following passage from his Convocation Address to the University of Lucknow read more like the utterance of a revolutionary than the polite platitudes of an academic orator, suggesting the political platform rather than the academic shades, the barricade rather than the cloister. "To my mind our country is to-day faced by a crisis of the first magnitude. It is not war or revolution or national bankruptcy, but internal disruption that is threatening us. The new India which we are attempting to build is being strangled at its very birth by anti-national forces. In the hour of our awakening we find ourselves surrounded by forces which make for our continual bondage. . . . If we are to preserve ourselves, we must use the lighted torch, the cleansing fire, the spirit that rebels. We must wrestle with the past that oppresses us, the relics of barbarism that threaten our very life, the fantastic notions about elemental facts that militate against decent living. We do things in our daily life which are a disgrace to our humanity. We eat food, wear clothes and enjoy comforts, while those who produce them are dying by degrees in unhealthy surroundings and bad economic conditions. We repress our natural sympathy with those who suffer because it does not pay us."

It ill becomes a stranger to expatiate upon the domestic affairs of a country which he has not visited and of which he is almost totally ignorant. Upon this aspect of Radhakrishnan's many-sided activities I, accordingly, refrain from comment.

I have given these extracts from his speeches in some little detail because they illustrate one side of the double rôle of their author as *liaison* officer between East and West.

THE *LIAISON* OFFICER

It is a side which will appear infrequently in the succeeding pages. Radhakrishnan, I am suggesting, is peculiarly fitted by nature and training to mediate between East and West. To quote from a review by Professor Muirhead of his Hibbert Lectures, *An Idealist View of Life*: "He has the rare qualification of being equally versed in the great European and the not less great Asiatic tradition which may be said to hold in solution between them the spiritual wisdom of the world, and of thus speaking as a philosophical bilinguist upon it."[1] It is as a philo-

[1] *Hibbert Journal*, October 1932.

sophical bilinguist that, while interpreting the
traditional wisdom of the East to compose the
current distraction of the West, he brings the force
and energy of the West to vitalize the apathy of
the East. His interpretation of Eastern philosophy
in its bearing upon the contemporary thought of
the West will form the main theme of this book.
It is, therefore, well that I should pause here to
point out with what enthusiastic zeal for reform,
in how impatient a spirit of protest Radhakrishnan
approaches the special problems of his own country.
This zeal for reform, this urgent spirit of protest
are the fruits of his contact with the West. They are
the expression of a personality who is a citizen not
only of his own country but of the world.

Radhakrishnan possesses the magic of intense
vitality. At his touch the dead bones of Indian lore
spring to new life. When he speaks of Indian
philosophy, or of the Hindu tradition, it is as if
a freshening wind blew through those musty
chambers whose walls are scored with sacred texts,
whose air is thick with the dust of dogma. The
shutters are opened and sun, air and light stream
into the room in whose corners has mouldered the
spirit of a dead past. "The Scriptures of an earlier
age" cannot, Radhakrishnan tells his countrymen,
"answer the problems of our time. The great
representatives of Indian culture were men of
mobility and ceaseless adventure, and we are not
loyal to their spirit if we mark time in a world of
perpetual movement by sitting still and chanting

ancient hymns. We cannot command the Sun to stand still in the plains of Hindustan."

INTERPRETATION OF INDIAN PHILOSOPHY

Vitality again is the distinguishing character of Radhakrishnan's interpretation of Indian philosophy. In an appendix to the first volume of his celebrated history, he indicates the ideals which have guided him in carrying out his undertaking. "The historian of philosophy," he says, "must approach his task, not as a mere philologist, or even as a scholar, but as a philosopher who uses his scholarship as an instrument to wrest from words the thoughts that underlie them."[1] What is the distinction? To the philologist the views of ancient thinkers are fossils to be recorded, catalogued and assigned to their appropriate thought-deposits. The endeavour to bring them to life he regards as irrelevant, even as inappropriate. To the philosopher they are significant only in so far as they throw light upon the problems of existence.

From this point of view the significance of Indian philosophy—at least of a highly creditable proportion of it—is perennial. It announces conceptions which, as we shall see later, reappear in modern thought with all the éclat of the latest speculative novelties. It is these conceptions which Radhakrishnan seeks to disinter from their antique settings and to make living to the modern reader. The task he describes as one of "creative logic," a task which involves not merely description and exposition, but

[1] *Indian Philosophy*, Vol. I, p. 671.

a constructive synthesis to effect which the synthesizer must "pay great attention to the logic of ideas, draw inferences, suggest explanations and formulate theories which would introduce some order into the shapeless mass of unrelated facts."[1]

The praise with which the critics greeted the appearance of Radhakrishnan's *Indian Philosophy* is the best testimony to the success with which he has carried out the task he has defined. I would recommend whoever is interested not merely in the past philosophy of India, but in the contemporary philosophy of the West, to read the concluding chapter of the second volume for a summary at once incisive and profound of those strands in the thought of India which, stretching from the remote past, are incorporated after more than four thousand years in the texture of the thought of the present. Looking back over the course which he has traversed, the record of which has covered more than fifteen hundred pages, Radhakrishnan considers whether there is any sense in which the development of Indian thought justifies the attribute "progressive." Impressed by the "beauty and the persistence" of this human effort continuing over four thousand years to understand, he is constrained, nevertheless, to emphasize how little is understood. That there is an ideal world, the home of the spirit, that spirit is primal and nature its creature and not vice versa— these things may be taken as agreed; but the limits of agreement are here reached.

[1] *Indian Philosophy*, Vol. I, p. 672.

Moreover, while the record is on the whole one of advance, the present, Radhakrishnan is constrained to admit, is, so far as Indian thought is concerned, an age of decadence. I shall return to this question in a later chapter. For the purposes of this one I am concerned merely to remark in this concluding chapter of his most substantial philosophical work the same strain of impatience with pedantry and mere scholarship, exaggerated respect for authority and reverence for the past which I have already noted in Radhakrishnan's political addresses. He roundly censures the writers on philosophy who "profess to be votaries of truth, though they understand by it merely the pious sophistries of the sacrosanct hair-splittings of this or that school of dogmatics."[1] It is not enough to know the thought of the past, we must develop it in the light of the present. Thus his countrymen are exhorted, "instead of resting content with the foundations nobly laid in the past," to "build a greater edifice in harmony with ancient endeavour as well as the modern outlook."[2]

SUSPECTED OPPOSITION TO RADHAKRISHNAN

Mankind has a habit of perpetually sweeping the dirt of its social abuses under the chairs and tables, where, since it is no longer visible, it is possible to pretend that it does not exist; and it is unfortunately a fact that, if somebody insists on sweeping it out

[1] *Indian Philosophy*, Vol. II, pp. 771, 772.
[2] Ibid., p. 768.

into the open again and bringing it to the notice of those whose business it is to remove it, they will be very angry with him and ten to one accuse him of having made it himself. The way of the social reformer is hard, and those who are unfortunate enough to be the vehicle of a message which the urge of life seeking expression drives them to communicate to their contemporaries, whether they want to listen to it or no, must be prepared for the hostility of vested interests in the thought of the past and the reputations of the present which will in all likelihood charge them with responsibility for the very abuses they denounce.

I should not, therefore, be surprised to learn that the new Hinduism is in certain quarters unpopular, and that Radhakrishnan, as one of its chief exponents, is not without his detractors. One cannot take in hand the task of rousing a people without rousing also the hostility of those who have neglected the job you are doing for them. One feels surprise less that Radhakrishnan should provoke opposition than that he should have provoked so little. I suggest in partial explanation a charm of manner which disarms opposition, while a persistent reasonableness removes its ground. That Radhakrishnan should arouse enthusiasm, which in the case of the young takes on an aspect of devotion, these things are in the nature of such men, and Radhakrishnan has fully lived up to the tradition of his kind. It is only this comparative absence of detraction that causes surprise.

CHAPTER II

COUNTER ATTACK

I. The Modern Criticism of Religion

HOSTILITY OF MODERN THOUGHT

Before I come to a statement of Radhakrishnan's positive philosophy I propose to give some account of his treatment, a highly significant treatment, of the prevailing modes of thought of the West. The first two chapters of his Hibbert Lectures, *An Idealist View of Life*, contain a brilliant and succinct statement of current Western 'isms.' Naturalism and Atheism, Agnosticism, Scepticism and Humanism, Pragmatism, Relativism and Modernism—all these are passed in rapid survey. Taken together they constitute a formidable attack upon the traditional religious view of the universe. The attack, supported by the Higher Criticism, reinforced by the study of Comparative Religion and equipped with the technique of psycho-analysis, has engendered an attitude of mind which is not so much actively hostile as passively indifferent to religion. It is often said that the contemporary mood of the West is one of doubt. This is not strictly true. Doubt at least implies interest in that which is doubted; but the average Westerner is not sufficiently interested either to doubt religion or to believe in it. For the most part, he simply does not think about the matter one way or the other.

For this attitude of casual indifference there are a number of causes, some of which I have endeavoured to examine in my *Present and Future of Religion*. Thought counts for little in the Western world, but it does count for a little, and among the causes must assuredly be included the influence of the various doctrines which are broadly denoted by the titles enumerated above. Now, however much these doctrines may differ in other respects, there is one point upon which all are in substantial agreement. This point is fatal to religion, and, unless it can be met, religion must be consigned to the scrap-heap to join magic, alchemy, astrology and those other toys of the spirit which, eagerly embraced in the childhood of the race, are discarded by its maturity.

The point may be stated as follows: Religion is not a statement of objective fact; it is merely a projection of human wishes. Primitive people 'animize' the forces of nature; projecting their personalities outside themselves, they attribute the causation of physical happenings to beings conceived more or less in their own image. There are gods in thunder, lightning and flood; there are gods for harvest and fertility. In due course the multitudes of primitive deities coalesce and become one. The process is sufficiently familiar and there is no need to dwell upon it here. Moreover, it still continues.

MAN IN THE UNIVERSE OF SCIENCE

Consider the insignificance of man, the tiny hold which he has upon space and time. The universe revealed to astronomy is very vast. What we already know is of unimaginable size, and what there may be beyond our telescopes we cannot tell. In the visible world the Milky Way is a fragment; in the Milky Way the solar system is a minute speck, and within the speck our planet is no more than a pin-point. On this pin-point tiny blobs of impure carbon and water of somewhat complicated structure and with somewhat unusual chemical properties move aimlessly about, until they are dissolved into the elements of which they are compounded. Such is the appearance which man's life presents to the point of view of the physical sciences.

Realizing his immense insignificance in this universe, whose vastness and indifference the advance of science only brings more depressingly home to him, and finding the realization intolerable, man creates a Being in his own image, elevates him to a position in the skies and then proceeds to endow him with every imaginable attribute of power and perfection, together with an insatiable interest in man's doings and an immense pity for his sufferings. Man has only to conceive himself as mattering to such a Being, and he has invested his life with the significance he desires. But the God so constructed is a figment; He is not *out there* in the world; He is projected by the mind of man upon the empty canvas of an indifferent universe. In fact, the universe is empty; it is mindless and purposeless, or, if it has a purpose, we do not know what it is. Finding the fact unbearable, we have insisted that the world is purposive and that the friendly and the spiritual underlie and condition the alien and the brutal.

RELIGION AS WISH FULFILMENT

The study of anthropology has shown us the process at work in primitive peoples; comparative religion testifies to its continuance in all times and places throughout man's recorded history; psycho-analysis has revealed its operations in ourselves. God, according to Freud, is a function of the unconscious invented to take the place of the father whose care, gratefully acknowledged in childhood, we miss in maturity. For the truth of the resultant beliefs, which are the stock-in-trade of religion, there is no evidence except our need to believe them true. It is, however, mere conceit to suppose that the universe exists to guarantee the fulfilment of our wishes. Hence, the universal desire of mankind to believe that God exists no more constitutes a reason for supposing that He does than the once universal belief that the earth is flat and situated in the centre of the heavens proved the facts of astronomy. We have, in fact, no right to suppose that the universe either corresponds to our aspirations or is conformable with our wishes. It follows that the religions of the world, valuable as psychology, are valueless as theology or philosophy. Telling us much about the heart of man, they tell us nothing about the universe. Their assertions have neither external reference nor objective validity; they are simply myths which man has made to comfort his loneliness.

Radhakrishnan sums up in his usual vivid phrases, "If the depths of the unconscious contain the dynamic drives, then ethical striving and religious aspiration are only illusions."[1] The fact of the matter is that "We are grown-up infants, and God is a sort of 'wet nurse' to humanity."[2]

This, then, is the charge, a charge which is brought forward as a necessary implication of the whole trend of modern science that Radhakrishnan has to meet. His answer consists of a rebuttal and a positive affirmation. I begin with the rebuttal, which itself falls into two parts.

II. The Rebuttal

RELIGION ASSERTS AN OBJECT

(a) First, religion involves definite knowledge and makes a definite affirmation. The universe, it affirms, is good; it is also spiritual; it is also in some sense personal. Of these facts we have direct and immediate experience. For some "the direct apprehension of God seems to be as real . . . as the perception of the external world is to others."[3] There

[1] *An Idealist View of Life,* p. 31.
[2] Ibid., p. 32.   [3] Ibid., p. 84.

is in us a "spiritual sense," an "instinct for the real,"[1] whose "milder forms are in the experience of all who feel an answering presence in deep devotion or share the spell which great works of art cast on us,"[2] but which ultimately will not be "satisfied with anything less than the absolute and the eternal."[3] Very well, then, religion *purports to be* an experience *of* something, knowledge *of* something, the expression of an instinct *for* something.

The charge is that the something, the *object* of the experience no less than the experience itself, originates in the experiencer; it is a part of his mind which he has projected outside himself in order to invest it with greater validity. And the answer is to ask why this charge should be brought against the object of religious knowledge but brought against no other? Why is our religious apprehension alone impugned in this way?

SENSE QUALITIES SUBJECTIVE

Consider, for example, the nature of our perception of the sensory world. On this vexed question Radhakrishnan takes an idealist line. He holds that the qualities and properties we believe ourselves to perceive in the world are not really out there waiting to be discovered by the human mind, but are relative to and dependent upon the observer, in the sense that they only exist as and when they are being experienced.

[1] *An Idealist View of Life*, p. 89.
[2] Ibid., p. 93.   [3] Ibid., p. 89.

"The sensible," he says, "is not the real," for it "is not," he continues, "independent of the observer. The colour of the rose exists only for one who has the human sense of sight. . . . Vibrations as much as colours are relative to the observer."[1] Radha-krishnan's view is not, however, the well-known position of Berkeley that the properties of the so-called external world are *merely* ideas in the mind of the observer. He holds rather that the distinction between subject and object, mind and external world, is one which in the last resort cannot be sustained. Knowledge is for him a whole or unity in which subject and object are both discerned as aspects of the unity; but this does not mean that either exists as a separate and isolated entity outside the unity of knowledge in which both are given. I shall return to this difficult point later. For the present it is sufficient to note that Radha-krishnan is an idealist, in that he does not believe that the qualities we perceive in the physical world are "out there" in the way in which common sense assumes, and that, like all idealists, he can produce very good reasons in support of his view.

IDEALIST TENDENCIES OF PHYSICS

If this is the case with regard to the world of common sense, it is not otherwise with the world of science. Science, it is common knowledge, has abandoned the nineteenth-century view according

[1] *An Idealist View of Life*, p. 193.

to which an external world consisting in the last analysis of little hard lumps of tangible substance, the atoms, was revealed to the mind of the enquiring scientist exactly as it was by a sort of divine revelation. To-day the nineteenth-century world of hard, tangible matter has been replaced by something infinitely elusive. It is variously described as a hump in space-time, a wave of probability undulating into nothingness, or as that which obeys certain differential equations. Its basis, the atom, has dissolved into charges of electricity which are not charges in anything. The atom, moreover, is never observed; it is merely inferred from the effects of its changes upon the surrounding spatio-temporal field. The laws governing its behaviour are not only unknown but in some respects appear to be contradictory. Where they can be affirmed with certitude, they turn out to be in the nature of statistical averages. More important still, physicists seem increasingly disposed to recognize the part played by the mind in determining the features of the physical world it seeks to catalogue. Sir Arthur Eddington regards the mind of the enquiring physicist as the chief architect of the world it knows; if it does not actually construct it, it arbitrarily selects it because of its measurable properties from the total context of the external world which is actually presented to the observer, while Sir James Jeans holds that matter is merely the way in which a fundamentally mental universe appears to our finite intelligences.

These views are not, of course, endorsed by all physicists. But on all sides there is a growing recognition of the part played by the mind in scientific work not only in discovering but in partially determining the nature of what it discovers, so that there is a tendency to think of the scientist as one who fares through the uttermost confines of the universe only to light upon his own footprints. But, if we do not know what matter is, if we have no assurance of the independent existence of an external physical world, either in the form in which everyday perception reveals it or in that into which the scientist analyses it, what standard have we by reference to which to stigmatize religious knowledge as *merely* subjective? That solid pedestal of simple, obvious matter which formed a point of vantage from which the nineteenth century looked down on the saint and the seer wandering in a world of moonshine has disappeared. Our religious intuitions have just as much right as any other form of knowledge to be accepted as giving us information about reality. "To say that our sense perceptions answer to reality, while our spiritual intuitions do not, is for psychology a gratuitous assumption. Psychologically the experience we have of the world before us, or of the British constitution or of the categorical nature of duty, is on the same level as St. Paul's vision on the road to Damascus or Augustine's in the Italian garden."[1]

[1] *An Idealist View of Life*, p. 85.

RELIGION, SCIENCE AND PERCEPTION ON ALL FOURS

This is not to say that the experiences in question, scientific as well as religious, are *all* subjective in the sense that they only introduce the subject to his own mental states; it is merely to argue that they are on all fours, and that any reason that there may be for stigmatizing religious experience as subjective applies with equal force to sense perception and scientific knowledge.

In fact, as I have already noted, Radhakrishnan is very far from being a *subjective* idealist. He holds that in all forms of experience something is given as object, but that the exact nature and properties of that object must remain unknown to us; or, rather, that, even if we can in some sense know the object intuitively, we cannot describe what we know. "We do not know precisely what matter or life is. We know that they are objects of experience though their real nature is hidden from us."[1] The further physics pushes its researches, the clearer does it become "that it is simply impossible to form any picture at all of the ultimate nature of the physical world. The theories are symbolic and are accepted because they work."[1] But just as we know that there is a world external to ourselves whose nature we are nevertheless unable to describe, so do we know that there is a God whose real nature is equally hidden from us. "We may know something about God or what answers to God in reality through

[1] *An Idealist View of Life*, p. 86.

religious experience."[1] This knowledge mankind has tried without much success to formularize in the different religions, just as the physicist tries to formularize his knowledge into theories. Thus "the creeds of religion correspond to theories of science. . . . We have certain experiences which we try to account for by the assumption of God,"[1] just as the scientist observes certain phenomena which he tries to account for by the assumption of the electron. "The God of our imagination may be as real as the electron,"[1] but both are only symbolic descriptions of a reality whose ultimate nature is unknown.

The first part of the rebuttal, therefore, takes the form of turning the critics' fire against themselves. 'If,' says Radhakrishnan in effect, 'there is any substance in your charge against religion, that it is *merely* subjective, then the charge applies equally well to science and to sense perception. In fact, you do not make it against the scientist (although the cap fits him particularly well at the moment) or against yourself as a common-sense man experiencing an everyday world. Why, then, make it against the man who enjoys religious experience?'

DIFFICULTIES OF SUBJECTIVISM

(*b*) While the first part of the rebuttal insists that religion has as good a right to claim objective validity as science without presuming to pronounce whether the right is a good one or not, the second insists that the right is in fact a good one. Radhakrishnan,

[1] *An Idealist View of Life*, p. 86.

I repeat, is not an extreme idealist who believes that the whole of what we know is the creation or projection of our own minds. Such a view cuts at the very root of all knowledge. For, if we suppose the object of knowledge to be *merely* subjective, a creation of the knowing mind or a copy or picture of an unknown reality outside it, then not only is the sense world destroyed but the world of science also goes by the board. If in perception I know only a private world owing all its features to the creative imagination of my mind, then, it is obvious, the world of my perception will be similarly limited. Each of us, therefore, will live in his own completely private world and we shall own no public world in common. Now science presupposes that there is some objective world which is the same for all discoverers, and a purely subjective Idealism robs science, therefore, of its basis.

That science is moonshine is, of course, possible, and, if this possibility were all, subjective Idealism might at least be countenanced as a plausible view. But there is more to follow. If what I perceive is the creation of my mind, so is what I think. Hence, what I think at any given moment will be wholly relative to me. Similarly, what you think will be wholly relative to you. Hence what you think may be the exact opposite of what I think, and yet it will not contradict it, since in each case what we think will be true in the only sense in which anything can be true, that is, it will be true for us.

Hence two contradictory thoughts may both be

true. To say that proposition 'X' is true means, in fact, on this view, no more than to say that I think 'X.' But, if the principle of contradiction does not hold, thought has no objective validity, since no assertion is truer than its opposite.

Very well, then, the argument which has led to this conclusion is no truer than its opposite, and there is no reason to accept the conclusion. We must, in fact, make some assertion; and, even if all we assert is a complete scepticism, we somehow regard the assertion of scepticism as being itself exempt from the scepticism which we proclaim in regard to other assertions. Thus, if I impugn the principle of contradiction, proclaiming a world in which two contrary assertions may both be true, I am cutting the ground from under my own feet, since in such a world my own thought will have no validity.

OUR ASPIRATIONS GROUNDED IN REALITY

From this *impasse* of a purely subjective Idealism Radhakrishnan is careful to guard himself. Certainly he does not wish to impugn the validity either of science or of thought; each, he holds, has external reference and gives us information about the world. But, if they do, so too does religion. Modern critics of religion have made a distinction between the faculty of reasoning employed by the scientist and the intuitive faculty of the mystic or seer. The former, they hold, gives information about an external world; the latter does not. But whence does the seer's faculty of insight arise? Clearly, if we are to take evolution seriously, we must grant that it has been evolved together with our other faculties. We are products of the evolutionary process; we are also determinate and integral factors of reality. It is not, therefore, reasonable to suppose that those intimations which in some degree we all possess, however much they may in practice be overlaid by the preoccupations of daily life, bear *no* relation to the universe which in producing us produced them. Whatever springs from the matrix of reality must reflect the origin from which it springs.

"Our sense perceptions, our logical concepts, our instinctive apprehensions, are not forms superinduced on reality, but are determinate forms of reality itself."[1]

Again, we grow up in constant contact with our environment. It determines to a large extent the colour of our mental as well as the facts of our bodily life. What we think at any given moment is at least in part a function of the environment in which we are placed. This impact of our environment upon us is a fact; our mental life consists in part of the series of responses which the impact generates, and our mental life includes our religious aspirations no less than our sensory experiences and trains of scientific reasoning. But, if this is the case, it is surely arbitrary to suppose that the aspirations in question reflect only *one* of the two sources from which they have so demonstrably sprung. As Radhakrishnan puts it, "The interaction of self

[1] *An Idealist View of Life*, p. 333.

and the universe has given rise to these aspirations, which are their joint products."[1] Hence, if we take our position as beings who are part and parcel of the process of nature seriously, we are not entitled to dismiss our religious aspirations, which are themselves the partial outcome of that process, as bearing no counterpart in nature. They must, Radhakrishnan holds, be thought to point to some feature in the universe which provokes and corresponds to them, and, because it corresponds, guarantees in some sense their fulfilment. The point here is really a double one.

THE OBJECT OF EXPERIENCE MUST BE REAL

First, our religious aspirations arise as a result of interaction between the self and the objective world external to the self; therefore, they have at least in part objective validity. Secondly, they assure us of the existence of something other than ourselves, which is presented to us for knowledge. "From the beginning we are in the presence of givenness, something experienced."[2] Admittedly, training and discipline may be needed to enable us to realize the nature of this 'something other'; we may for lack of them be blind. But "because the objects are perceived only when our minds are trained, it does not follow that the objects are subjective. To see a rose we must turn our eyes in that direction. To realize the supreme spirit, a certain purifying of the

[1] *An Idealist View of Life*, p. 333.
[2] Ibid., p. 334.

mind is necessary."[1] In other words, the fact that many in the modern world would appear to lack the religious sense, or, at least, seem disposed to deny its object, is no more a reason for regarding its object as illusory than the fact that human beings cannot hear sound waves of more than a certain frequency of vibration is a reason for supposing that higher frequencies of vibration do not occur.

Hence, the second part of the rebutting case introduces a tincture of Realism to qualify the Idealism of the first. Radhakrishnan first shows that neither in perception nor in science nor in religion can we suppose that the object of the human mind is something which, existing in independence of our knowing it, is revealed to us exactly as it is. He then proceeds to affirm that nevertheless there is an object. Something is given external to ourselves which we know in religion, just as something is given external to ourselves which we know in science. This, according to Radhakrishnan, is the essence and core of the time-honoured ontological argument for the existence of God. It is not a case of saying 'I have an idea of perfection; therefore' (as a logical inference) 'perfection must exist, in order to account for my idea of it'; the point is rather that the experience of having the idea inevitably involves the experience of the object of which it is an idea.[2]

---

[1] *An Idealist View of Life*, p. 334.
[2] See ibid., pp. 220–221.

SUMMARY OF LOGICAL ARGUMENT

Given the validity of the preceding argument, the argument, namely, to show "that our deepest convictions give us trustworthy knowledge of ultimate reality"[1] in just the same way as science and sense experience give us knowledge of reality, then it follows that, just in so far as we have some idea of ultimate reality—and most of us do in fact have *some* idea—then that idea is evidence that we have been "in immediate cognitive relation"[1] with its object. In other words, an intuitive consciousness of God is (still assuming that we accept the validity of the foregoing logical argument) a necessary presupposition of the idea of Him. Do we in fact have this intuitive consciousness?

ABSENCE OF RELIGIOUS CONSCIOUSNESS IN WEST

At this point in the argument the Western reader will do well to pay attention; for it is, I believe, a simple statement of psychological fact that, whereas most of the peoples of the world have in some form or other had this consciousness, most people in the West to-day have not. As a consequence religion means nothing to them, simply because they are without that basis of personal experience in terms of which alone religion has meaning. Now this lack is, I believe, a comparatively new thing in the world. Radhakrishnan simply does not credit its existence. He speaks as if the religious consciousness were an

[1] *An Idealist View of Life*, p. 220.

inalienable and universal possession of the human spirit, something which all human beings enjoy in so far as they are in fact human. I can only say that I have looked into my consciousness very carefully and can find nothing of the kind, unless, as Radhakrishnan suggests, I am prepared to accept my feeling for Nature and the "spell" which great "works of art cast upon us" as religious. Although I cannot do this—I think that the feeling one has for great art, though possibly akin to, is different from that of which the mystics speak; for example, when I enjoy a Bach fugue I do not in any sense become it; yet most mystics insist that in religious ecstasy the gulf between subject and the object which they enjoy is transcended and that they become one with the object—I am none the less grateful to a love of music for providing me with a helpful analogy in this matter. I admire Bach's music more than I can say and consider its composer to be the greatest man who ever lived.

ANALOGY FROM MUSICAL APPRECIATION

Now this admiration has, from the psychological point of view, two interesting characteristics. First, I am quite sure that I am right to have it; it carries with it, that is to say, an absolute certitude as to the objective admirableness of its object; secondly, I am completely unable to communicate my admiration to others, or to explain why Bach is great. In respect of its first characteristic my feeling for Bach is unlike my love of mushrooms and lobsters, and like my conviction that two and two make four. In respect of its second, its incommunicableness, it is unlike my mathematical knowledge and akin to my partialities of taste; that is to say, when people pester me to explain what it is that I can see in Bach, I can no more answer them than I can answer them when they ask for reasons for the preferences of my palate. Nor is this failure due to any marked deficiency in my powers of exposition.

Now it seems to me that the attitude adopted to their own experiences by those who enjoy an intuitive consciousness of God is very like my attitude to Bach. Equally they are convinced, convinced that they have experienced a surpassing beauty and an overwhelming goodness; but they cannot communicate that of which they are convinced. Hence, despite my own lack of such experience, I am no more disposed to doubt the truth of what they say than I expect others to doubt the excellence of Bach, or am myself disposed to deny that there are sounds caused by vibrations above a certain frequency merely because my auditory apparatus does not permit me to hear them. Nor is my case unrepresentative of the present generation in the West, although it might quite well have been so at almost any previous period in the history of civilization.

I have recently engaged in a controversy on the truth of Christianity with an eminent writer who maintained the absolute and exclusive truth of the Christian religion. I expected him to take his stand on personal experience, proclaiming a faith which was based upon a revelation which he had individually enjoyed. I actually went out of my way to warn him not to take this line, pointing out that, even if personal revelation was a trump card for those who had enjoyed it, it could take no tricks from those who had not. His reply effectively took the wind out of my controversial sails. Completely disclaiming any *personal* experience of God, he asserted a faith based not upon intuition but upon reason. His reason was, he said, convinced by the evidence for the Virgin Birth and the Resurrection of the Divinity of Christ. This being so, it seemed to him reasonable to accept on *faith* the doctrines which the Church as the divinely appointed expositor of Christian teaching laid down.[1] I mention the case both in order to illustrate the comparative absence of direct first-hand religious experience in the West, and also to emphasize the fact that this absence does not *in itself* afford any valid ground for rejecting the testimony of those who have enjoyed it.

Now that I have done my best to cut the ground from under the feet of the anti-religious prejudices of Western readers, I come to the positive statement of Radhakrishnan's case, which turns upon the nature and testimony of religious experience.

[1] See *Is Christianity True?* a series of letters between the present author and Arnold Lunn. (Eyre and Spottiswood, 7s. 6d.)

III. The Affirmation

THE RAW MATERIAL OF RELIGION

Religious experience is, Radhakrishnan points out, the beginning of all religion. "All the religions owe their inspiration to the personal insights of their prophet founders."[1] It also provides its raw material, standing to religious belief as the experimental data of the physicist stand to the formulae in which he sums up and the theories by which he seeks to interpret them. "If philosophy of religion is to become scientific, it must become empirical and found itself on religious experience.[2]

The existence of this raw material of religion is a matter of fact; with some men it is a continuous fact, in most only intermittent. "The direct apprehension of God seems to be as real to some men as the consciousness of personality or the perception of the external world is to others. The sense of communion with the divine, the awe and worship which it evokes, which to us are only moments of vision or insight, seem to be normal and all-pervading with the saints."[2]

What are the characteristics of this experience? First, it is an experience of *something*; it is not, that is to say, purely subjective. We have, as we have seen, no more reason to doubt the existence of an object of religious experience than we have that of

[1] *An Idealist View of Life*, p. 89.
[2] Ibid., p. 84.

a molecule or a rose. Certainly the person enjoying it has no doubts. "In the experience itself no question is raised whether the object experienced is real or not."[1] Secondly, it is not an experience on the part of any single sense or faculty but of the whole being or personality. It acts, therefore, as an integrator of the various parts or aspects of the personality, so that in religious experience alone we become whole men, and not a more or less unified bundle of faculties and desires: "We reach the religious object by the totality of our faculties and energies."[2] It is precisely this functioning of the whole that men have intended to convey by the phrase "spiritual life." Man is more truly spirit than he is mind or body, because it is only when all his faculties are integrated into a whole which transcends any of them, only when by virtue of such integration he realizes all that he has it in him to be, that he functions spiritually.

RELIGIOUS INSIGHT AND THE UNCONSCIOUS

It is worth while pausing to emphasize at this point the distinction between religious experience and the functioning of the unconscious which figures so prominently in the literature of psycho-analysis. As will be seen when I come to Radhakrishnan's account of the faculty by means of which religious experience is enjoyed, a faculty which for want of a better word he terms 'Intuition,' there are two important features in common between the intuitional con-

[1] *An Idealist View of Life*, p. 85.
[2] Ibid., p. 88.

sciousness and the psycho-analyst's unconscious. First, both are commonly and correctly referred to by such words as immediate, dynamic, non-logical, non-intellectual. In the second place, both the intuitional consciousness and the unconscious are regarded as constituting the very core and essence of the individual, the seat of personality, the citadel of the self, the modern substitute for what in old-fashioned language man has called his soul.

Yet between the contemporary Freudian conception of the unconscious as the "condition in which desires stimulated by our nature but rejected by our normal consciousness, exist in all their potency waiting for opportunities to overthrow the censor,"[1] and the spiritual core of the religious consciousness there is a world of difference. And this difference may most conveniently be expressed by reference to the concept of wholeness or integration of personality which is now being emphasized. In integrating the personality religious experience includes and transcends both consciousness and the unconscious. "The great insights which surprise us by their strangeness and significance are born not of the unconsciousness but of the spirit in us, the self in its entirety which includes both the conscious and the unconscious."[1] This integrated self which enjoys religious experience "is not the asylum of outlawed desires, but is the essential unique nature of each individual creature."[2]

[1] *An Idealist View of Life*, pp. 215, 216.
[2] Ibid., p. 216.

F

Thirdly, religious experience effects this integration of parts into a whole because it is a response or reaction *to a whole*. Aesthetic enjoyment is our response to the beauty of the universe, moral experience to its goodness, science to its natural facts; but religious experience is at once our awareness of and response to that whole of which beauty, goodness and fact are aspects or manifestations. And, just as the response "unifies all values and organizes all experiences"[1] in the spirit responding, so does that for which the response is felt unify and integrate all the different aspects of being which are studied in the various departments of man's thought and enjoyed in the various aspects of his multiform activity. If the word 'aesthe' could revert to its original meaning, robbed of the unfortunate *nuances* with which the excesses of the *fin de siècle* movement in Europe invested it, we might say that the mystic is the aesthete of the universe.

SELF-TRANSCENDENCE

Fourthly, not only are the ideas, feelings and faculties of the individual fused into a unity of experience, but that unity is extended to embrace the object of the experience. Radhakrishnan fully endorses the almost unanimous testimony of the great Christian mystics, that in mystical experience the boundary between the self and the not self is crossed and the self, transcending the limitations

[1] *An Idealist View of Life*, p. 88.

of its own finitude, passes beyond itself to merge with its object. "Consciousness and being," he says, "are not there different from each other. . . . Thought and reality coalesce and a creative merging of subject and object results. . . . In this fullness of felt life and freedom, the distinction of the knower and the known disappears."[1] From Radhakrishnan this statement is not invested with quite the significance which it would have, if it were made by a realist or by one who held a common-sense theory of knowledge, and this for two reasons. First, Radhakrishnan, as we have seen, regards every process of knowing of whatever type as a fusion in which knower and known are merged in a unity.[2] Secondly, he holds that the human consciousness is in any event continuous with reality; that reality is, in fact, the core of our being and God already in our hearts. This being so, to know reality, or to enter in communion with God, is in a very literal sense to realize oneself. I shall return to this point in Chapter IV.[3] For the present it is worth while pointing out that these two considerations considerably modify the character of uniqueness which one would normally, in the light of Radhakrishnan's account, be justified in claiming for religious experience. All experience must, it seems, for Radhakrishnan, be in some degree religious.

Withal the religious experience is one of peace and great joy. The cares of life vanish; its preoccupations disappear; the toothaches and pimples of

[1] *An Idealist View of Life*, p. 92.   [2] See p. 65.   [3] See p. 136.

our daily experience are seen in their proper perspective; the experience, in fact, is profoundly satisfying. Not only does it satisfy; it alters. It alters the natures of those who enjoy it; nor does the alteration fade with the experience but persists, bringing a permanent enrichment of the whole being.

SUMMARY OF CHARACTERISTICS OF
RELIGIOUS EXPERIENCE

I cannot do better than sum up this brief account by quoting an eloquent passage from Radhakrishnan's *An Idealist View of Life*.

"It does not come in a fragmentary or truncated form demanding completion by something else. It does not look beyond itself for meaning or validity. It does not appeal to external standards of logic or metaphysics. It is its own cause and explanation. It is sovereign in its own rights and carries its own credentials. It is self-established (svatassiddha), self-evidencing (svasamvedya), self-luminous (svayam-prakāśa). It does not argue or explain but it knows and is. It is beyond the bounds of proof and so touches completeness. It comes with a constraint that brooks no denial. It is pure comprehension, entire significance, complete validity."[1]

To command this experience and to retain it at will would be heavenly. It is, indeed, the continuance of the experience which constitutes dwelling in Heaven, "which is not a place where God lives, but a mode of being which is fully and completely real."[2]

[1] *An Idealist View of Life*, pp. 92, 93.   [2] Ibid., p. 93.

THE EXPERIENCE NEITHER TO BE SUMMONED
NOR RETAINED

In fact, however, even the most gifted human souls are unable to command their moments of spiritual revelation and enjoyment. And they cannot do this because, beyond recognizing the need for silence and for meditation, for a discipline of life and a training of the spirit of which I shall speak later,[1] mankind has hitherto been quite unable to specify the conditions governing the occurrence of these experiences: "We do not know how or why they occur. They sometimes occur even against our will."[2]

It is, alas, a fact that, although within limits we can command the experience of pleasant bodily sensations and can even, within limits, ensure the gratifications of the mind, the experiences of the spirit cannot be summoned at will. I know that with a clean palate I shall always appreciate strawberries and green peas, and can be soothed in body and mellowed in mind by a good claret followed by port; I know even that, whatever my mood, certain Prefaces of Shaw will stimulate me, certain Dialogues of Plato delight me, certain Essays of Charles Lamb or W. H. Hudson give me solace and repose. But I cannot command my pleasure in music. How often have I been to a concert at which the most delicious pieces of Bach and Mozart were played, and come away baffled and bewildered at

[1] See pp. 148–150, 158. [2] *An Idealist View of Life*, p. 94.

my lack of enjoyment, so that I have set to wondering whether I had lost the capacity for my greatest pleasure! As it is with musical, so I understand it to be with religious experience.

And, as it cannot be summoned, religious experience cannot be retained. "So long as the experience lasts, the individual remains rapt in contemplation, but no man can rest in that state for all time. Life is a restless surge. Scarcely is the seer assured of the unique character of the experience than he is caught in the whirl of desire and temptation, discord and struggle."[1]

Radhakrishnan's words are a plain record of a fact, a fact to which all who have enjoyed aesthetic as well as religious experience will testify. I have often puzzled over this tantalizing aspect of man's relation to reality, and, if I may be permitted to quote what I have written elsewhere, I propose to insert here a short passage from my *Philosophical Aspects of Modern Science* which, allowing for some slight change in terminology, seems to me exactly to express Radhakrishnan's point of view.

"The awareness of value cannot at our present stage of evolution be more than a fleeting and uncertain experience; like thinking in a dog, it is a mode of apprehension to which the species has only just attained. It is still an abnormal capacity, exercised not continuously at the level of everyday experience, but enjoyed in fleeting and tantalizing glimpses of a world not normally accessible to

[1] *An Idealist View of Life*, p. 94.

consciousness. The soul of man, if I may resort to a metaphor, is like a chrysalis maturing in the cocoon of matter, from which one day it will burst forth and spread its wings in the sun of pure reality. In the appreciation of art which is a foretaste of our knowledge of reality, the soul is, as it were, torn prematurely from its cocoon and subjected to experiences of a quality and intensity for which it is as yet insufficiently prepared.

"For the world of value is a shining glory, the direct vision of which man is unable as yet to endure. Yet the glory shines through the veil of sense and the alert and receptive mind catches its reflection in common things. The artist and the musician are seekers after that glory, and the haunting beauty that they pursue is the reflection of its light. At times they may even catch a glimpse of the original itself, and, seeing it, are transported with delight. But their vision, if indeed they have it, is never more than a fleeting glimpse. For a continuous vision the soul of man is not as yet prepared. Faced with a direct view of reality, it falters and falls back, and, were not the veil of matter mercifully interposed, it would be stunned and blinded by the force and glory of reality; thus it must content itself with images. It is this inability of the soul to prolong or to maintain the awareness of value that suggests a clue to the interpretation of much that is puzzling in aesthetic experience, whether regarded as creative or appreciative."[1]

[1] Joad, *Philosophical Aspects of Modern Science*, pp. 301, 302.

ORIGIN OF RELIGIOUS CREEDS

I proceed to suggest that it is to this same inability to retain our deepest and most illuminating experiences that we must look for an explanation of the artist's creation. Why, it might be asked, should the artist create at all? He does so, I surmise, that he may have a souvenir to remind him of an experience he can no longer retain. Creation is a testimony not to present inspiration, but to inspiration which, once enjoyed, has now failed.

Radhakrishnan invokes the same consideration to account for the existence of religious creeds and for their diversity. When the period of subsequent reflection upon the experience begins, the seer who has enjoyed the revelation feels convinced of its truth. Further experience is not wanted to confirm, rational criticism cannot avail to shake his sense of certainty. "Doubt and disbelief are no more possible."[1] Hence the simplicity and directness of the utterances of the great religious seers, of the author of the Upanisads, of Christ, of Buddha, Eckhart or Blake.

But the experience from its very nature is incommunicable. Language was created to convey the meanings of this world; it cannot readily be applied to the uses of another. It is not to be supposed that mind can communicate its vision of reality in symbols appropriate to the world of appearance. If mysticism could give an account of itself, it

[1] *An Idealist View of Life,* p. 95.

would cease to be mysticism. Yet convinced of the immense significance of his vision, irradiated by its splendour, the seer is unable to keep silent: "Though the tools of sense and of understanding cannot describe adequately, creative imagination with its symbols and its suggestions"[1] may serve. Hence the insight of the original religious geniuses, the expression by which Radhakrishnan designates the mystics, is conveyed to us in the language of "myths and metaphors," and, we may add, of parables. And from the very fact that myths, metaphors and parables have no fixed meaning, they may be "interpreted as life requires."[1] Different ages employ different concepts; they also have different needs; hence, when the process of interpretation begins, we find the date afforded by the revelatory insight of the religious genius interpreted in terms of different concepts and used to justify different beliefs. There arises, as a result, a multiplicity of religious creeds, various, contradictory and, because contradictory, warring. Yet the number and variety of religious creeds no more invalidate the reality of the experience and the authenticity of the vision of the universe which the experience suggests, than the fact that a dozen painters render a landscape in a dozen different ways entitles us to conclude that each picture represents a different scene, or even that it represents no scene at all.

[1] *An Idealist View of Life*, p. 97.

THE PERSONAL EXPERIENCE AND THE
    INTERPRETATIVE CREED

Thus an important distinction arises in the sphere of what is loosely called religious experience or religious knowledge, neglect of which, reinforced by the bigotry which claims exclusive truth for particular creeds, is responsible for much of the contemporary confusion of religions and, in particular, for the disrepute into which in the West religion has fallen.

A. First, there is the fact of religious experience. This is in the nature of an instinctive flash, rarely of a prolonged vision, which may be led up to but is logically divorced from the years of personal training and centuries of collective tradition that may precede it. The knowledge that this flash conveys cannot be directly communicated, but, if the unanimity of all the great religious mystics on this point may be taken as evidence, we may say that it conveys an assurance of three things. First, "the soul is in contact with a mighty spiritual power other than its normal self."[1] Secondly, this spiritual power is nevertheless within itself. Thirdly, the "contact means the beginning of the creation of a new self."[1]

B. Following upon the fact, there is the interpretation of the fact. The process of interpretation itself falls into two stages. (1) First, there is *some* tincture of interpretation even in the experience itself. Radhakrishnan is in line with most modern

[1] *An Idealist View of Life*, p. 99.

psychology in pointing out that "there is no such thing as pure experience raw and undigested. It is always mixed up with layers of interpretation."[1] Buddha, of all the teachers who have manifestly enjoyed the experience, was the most chary of interpreting it. For him the view that "the experience gives us direct contact with God is an interpretation and not an immediate datum."[2] But even Buddha interprets, when he tells us that the world of the spirit penetrates and underlies the sensible world. And the point is that the form which the interpretation takes depends not only upon the nature of the experience but also and for most of its characteristic features upon the temperament, education, training and world outlook of the experiencer.

(2) This is even truer of the second stage. The revelation of the founder has now to filter through the minds of followers who are for the most part very ordinary men. No man can understand the teaching of another; all that he can do is to understand the nearest thing to it of which his own mind is capable, and the nearest thing to the teaching of the founder of a religion of which the average follower is capable is something very remote indeed, amounting in the case of Paul to the transformation of the original and highly advanced teaching of Jesus into a commonplace mixture of repentance, retribution and salvationism. Hence the variety of

---

[1] *An Idealist View of Life*, p. 99.
[2] Ibid., p. 100.

religious beliefs; hence, too, the fact that the average man associates his own particular religious experience with the name and often attributes it to the agency of some one particular founder, and proceeds to interpret it in the context of some one particular creed determined by the accident of the time and place in which he happens to have entered the world. This does not mean, as some seem to think it does, that one's religion is *purely* a topographical accident, its character and intensity depending upon the bedroom in which one happens to have been born. It does mean, in Radhakrishnan's words, that "the identification" of the spiritual reality of the universe "with the historic figures of Buddha or Christ, the confusion of the simple realization of the universal self in us with a catastrophic revelation from without, is an interpretation, a personal confession and not necessarily an objective truth."[1]

THE ANSWER TO RELATIVISM

Here, then, is the gist of Radhakrishnan's answer to the modern relativist criticism of religion. Certainly, he says, there are different creeds. But what does the circumstance prove? Merely that there are different interpretations of a fundamentally unitary experience. Admittedly, again, the features which different religions display to the world are local, parochial even, and relative to circumstances of time and place. But what does that show? Simply that the deliverances of religious insight have to be

[1] *An Idealist View of Life*, p. 99.

interpreted through the partial, relative and faulty minds of men.

But this is only to surmount our first hurdle; the second presents itself with the question, 'How far can the implications of these deliverances be reconciled with the facts of experience and the demands of reason? How far, in fact, do they require a view of the universe and of the function and status of human life within it, which is on other grounds acceptable?' Or, to put the question in another way, 'What sort of universe must this universe be in order that these deliverances may be accepted as significant in the present and vindicated in the future? And is this the sort of universe which from other points of view it does in fact seem to be?'

These are the questions which Radhakrishnan seeks to answer by means of a positive system of metaphysics and a consequential doctrine of ethics. The answer will be given in two later chapters. Before coming to them I propose to include a short account of Radhakrishnan's treatment of the faculty by means of which religious experience is obtained, a treatment which affords a particularly good example of his *flair* for combining new Western knowledge with traditional Eastern wisdom.

CHAPTER III

INTUITION

CHANGE IN WESTERN THOUGHT

The East has always taught that man is in his inmost being a spirit, and that it is in virtue of his spiritual nature that he responds to and may ultimately become one with spiritual reality, whether conceived as personal God or as impersonal Absolute. The West has been inclined to concede for some time past that reasoning is not living; it is not even knowing: at any rate it is not *all* that we mean by knowing. Of so much, at least, psycho-analysis has convinced us, demonstrating, as Radhakrishnan points out, that "living experience is more extensive than logical reasoning. The roots of life are in the unconscious depths of the soul."[1] But, if reason is not the whole of life, still less is it the whole of knowledge. The intellectual ratiocinative faculty employed by the scientist and the practical man is not, we are beginning to recognize, the only instrument by means of which the human mind may come to know the world or to achieve truth. The method of science, it is increasingly realized, is to analyse and take to bits; therefore it deals with and gives information not about wholes but about parts. From the 'wholeness' in which they are given, the parts are isolated and considered in their

[1] *An Idealist View of Life*, p. 217.

rôle of parts only by an act of abstraction, which, when taken as giving a true and complete account of what is abstracted, is seen to be vicious. Science, then, it is urged, cannot give us information about the reality of things.

Let us take a concrete example of the way in which this recognition may be applied to a particular case. I take a case in which *on any view* the reality of a thing resides most palpably in the whole rather than in the parts, the case of individuality, and more particularly of that kind of individuality which in human beings we know as personality.

THE SCIENTIFIC ACCOUNT OF PERSONALITY

Let us suppose that the various accounts which can be given of the human organism were to be enumerated and collated. We should begin, say, with the physiological account in terms of tubes and pipes, nerves and bones and blood vessels. These, presumably, can be analysed into their chemical compounds, and there is, therefore, a chemical account in terms of molecules and elements. These, again, can be analysed in terms of their atomic constituents, and there is, therefore, the physicist's account in terms of protons and electrons. Beginning at the other end of the scale, we should have to include the psychologist's account in terms of mental events, images, sensations and so forth, with special departmental accounts such as the behaviourist's in terms of language habits and conditioned reflexes, and the psycho-analyst's in terms of unconscious desire and promptings of the libido. From other points of view there is the economic man and the *median* man of the statistician; there is man from the standpoint of the biologist and man as he appears to the anthropologist. There is also the account of particular individual men to be found in the works of a great novelist. Each of these accounts could in theory be made accurate and complete—complete, that is to say, so far as it goes; yet each would be couched in different terms. To say that no one of these accounts conveys the whole truth about a man, but describes only some particular aspect of him which has been selected for special attention, would be to state a commonplace.

But more than this is implied in the current criticism of scientific method as concerned with abstractions. It is implied that, if all the different accounts, the physiological, the chemical, the physical, the psychological, the behaviouristic, the psycho-analytic, the economic, the statistical, the biological, the anthropological and the novelist's, were collated, supplemented with other accurate and complete but partial accounts and worked up into a comprehensive survey, they would still fail to constitute *the* truth about a man. And they would fail to do this, not because some particular piece of information had been left out, or some particular point of view forgotten—for, it would be urged, no matter how complete the collection of scientific

is reached is independent of this process of later rationalization, which is irrelevant to the truth of the conviction. Reached by non-rational processes, although it may be subsequently defended by rational ones, an intuitive conviction must carry its guarantee of authenticity within itself. The basis of all reasoning process is, it is generally agreed, similarly intuitive; but we do not distrust mathematics because its premises are undemonstrated.

(3) Instead of standing outside, intuition enters into its object and by sympathy becomes temporarily one with it. Bergson describes intuition as "the kind of intellectual sympathy by which one places oneself within an object in order to coincide with what is unique in it and therefore inexpressible."[1]

THE PROCESS OF ARTISTIC CREATION

Let us take as an illustration of this particular aspect of intuition the procedure of the great artist. The great artist, it is said, penetrates through the superficial appearance presented by his subject to the reality beneath: it is, in fact, his vision of this reality that constitutes his greatness as an artist. This vision he places upon canvas, and it is in the truth of the vision and not in the paint, the colours, the form, the technique, or the faithful portrayal of the subject that the essence of the picture lies. And just as it is only by entering by sympathy into the meaning of his subject that the artist

[1] Bergson, *Introduction to Metaphysics*, E.T., p. 6.

succeeds in grasping it, so, by analogy, it is through the intellectual sympathy, which is intuition, that we are enabled to enter into the nature of the reality which underlies the phenomenal appearances of science and of sense.

If appreciation of great art implies an entering of the spirit into the reality of that which is appreciated, the affectionate knowledge of a personality involves, it is said, a yet higher and more intimate degree of communion. The fact is testified by the metaphors of common language. We speak of "entering into the mind and heart of a friend," and of "the community of heart and soul" which is said to be one of the distinguishing marks of true lovers. To love nature is "to be at one with her," and God is worshipped in "Oneness of spirit." We may go further and think of two persons intimately acquainted and deeply loving each other as creating a new spiritual unity, a common soul, as it were, in which the separate personality of each is fused and by which it is transcended. There is much in the writings of the mystical poets to lend countenance to this conception.

(4) Fourthly, the intuitional faculty is said to be a natural human attribute, as natural and universal as the sense of sight and hearing, so that, lacking it, a person may be justifiably regarded as being in virtue of his lack not fully and completely a human being.

(5) It is, finally, pre-eminently the faculty which assures us of the meaning and significance of things,

so that without its assurance we should be justified in concluding that the universe is, as it appears to mechanistic science, without point or purpose. Nor is it only of meaning and significance that it assures us, but of a divine meaning and a personal significance. I will take a quotation from Professor Eddington to illustrate these last two points. "There are some to whom the sense of a divine presence irradiating the soul is one of the most obvious things of experience. *In their view a man without this sense is to be regarded as we regard a man without a sense of humour. The absence is a kind of mental deficiency.*"[1] (My italics.)

Now I have summarized this view of intuition, a view increasingly prevalent in Western thought, because it might stand *mutatis mutandis* for Radhakrishnan's own account of the spiritual faculty by means of which we enjoy religious experience.

THE PSYCHOLOGISTS ON INTUITION

In recent years much work has been done in investigating what might be called the psychological machinery of intuition, the conditions under which it operates, its relation to intellectual effort, the verifiability of its deliverances by subsequent test.

An interesting summary of this research will be found in Graham Wallas's book *The Art of Thought*. He distinguishes four stages in the process which goes to the making of a new generalization, the dis-

[1] Eddington, *The Nature of the Physical World*, p. 322.

covery of a new formula or the devising of a new invention. The first is that of Preparation, during which a particular problem is investigated in all directions; the second, that of Incubation, during which no conscious thinking is done in connection with the problem of work or art with which the creative thinker or artist is concerned; the third, consisting of the appearance of the "happy idea," together with the psychological events accompanying that appearance, is called Illumination; and the fourth, embodying the working out and application of the idea in thought or in the execution of the work of art, Verification.

Particular stress is laid upon the importance of Preparation as a preliminary to Illumination. Professor Wallas speaks of the many men of genius who have done their best work after a period of idleness.[1] But the period of idleness must itself be preceded by a spell of hard thinking, during which the intellect is working at full pressure. To adopt the language of modern psychology, we may say that consciousness during the thinking stage propounds a problem, collects the relevant data and explores different avenues for a possible solution. A period of rest ensues during which the problem and relevant data are transferred to the unconscious. That the unconscious may work effectively, consciousness must so far as possible be unoccupied. The solution is worked out by the unconscious, and appears in due course as the "happy idea"

[1] Wallas, *The Art of Thought*, pp. 88–91.

of the scientist and the inspiration of the artist. The "happy idea" which succeeds the period of hard thinking is of an entirely different order from the thinking itself. It outruns thinking and, although it is led up to, is far from being necessitated by it. The mind, in other words, makes a definite jump, after the process of logical thought is completed, and it is for this reason that in the sphere of science a subsequent process of Verification is necessary.

THE PROGRESS OF AESTHETIC INSIGHT

That this 'jumping' on the part of the mind is an integral factor in the intuitional process is now fairly widely recognized by the Western consciousness in connection with aesthetic experience, a brief account of which will serve to illustrate Radhakrishnan's theory of intuition in the form in which it will be most intelligible to those of us in the West who have lost the faculty of religious insight. The *locus classicus* for such an account is Plato's *Symposium*, where the voyage of the mind in search of beauty is described. The mind, Plato holds, does not apprehend beauty all at once, but passes through an ordered progression of gradually increasing aesthetic insight. Plato follows the course of the mind from the apprehension of the beauty of one beautiful object to that of many, through the abstract beauty of morals and concepts to the vision of absolute beauty, the Form itself. Practice in apprehension at each level of the process prepares the mind for apprehension at the next. And it does this partly because the objects apprehended at each stage possess the property of directing the mind's attention to the next. Not only is the function of education to wheel the soul "round from the perishing world" to "the contemplation of the real world and the brightest part thereof,"[1] but the visible world itself possesses the power of "turning the eye of the soul" towards the intelligible. But just as between the two worlds there is fixed a gulf, the gulf between 'becoming' and 'being,' so from the apprehension of the one to the apprehension of the other there is a definite jump.

Now this mental jump is, it seems to me, a plain fact of aesthetic experience. You look at a tree on many occasions and notice it only as possible timber, or as an elm, or as dangerous; or you do not notice it at all. Then comes a day when you *suddenly* notice that it is beautiful. . . . It is the same with a picture; its beauty *suddenly* strikes us.

RADHAKRISHNAN'S ENDORSEMENT

The above constitutes a brief and summary account of the development of the intuitive spirit, as it discovers new truth in science, creates new beauty in art and newly apprehends the beauty of nature. At every stage of this account appropriate quotations from Radhakrishnan could have been given, emphasizing the characteristic features of this same intuitional activity as it is enjoyed in *religious* experience. "The experience is felt as of the nature of a discovery

[1] *Republic*, vii, 518.

or a revelation, not a mere conjecture or creation.
The real was there actually confronting us. . . ."[1]
And the knowledge which the discovery brings is
"an immediate and intuitive certainty transcending
any which mere reason can reach."[1] "Ideas which
seem to come to us with compelling force, without
any mediate intellectual process of which we are
aware, are generally the results of previous training
in traditions imparted to us in our early years. Our
past experience supplies the materials to which the
new insight adds fresh meanings."[2] Clearly a description of 'Preparation'! "Intellectual inaction seems to
be the prelude to the intuitive flash. To allow the
non-intellectual and yet rational part of our mind
to play on the subject, relaxation is necessary. . . .
We must allow the intellect to lie fallow, let the
object soak into the subsoil of our mental life and
elicit its reaction to it."[3] Obviously an account of
'Incubation.' And so on; each stage in the process
outlined above could similarly be illustrated with
its appropriate quotation.

THE MORAL FOR WESTERN THOUGHT

Now the point which I wish to emphasize is that
in these passages Radhakrishnan is writing not of
art but of religion; he is describing the nature of
the consciousness by means of which religious truth
is apprehended and religious insight enjoyed. My
account bore reference to science and art; it was

[1] *An Idealist View of Life*, p. 95.
[2] Ibid., p. 98.   [3] Ibid., p. 179.

an account of the process by which scientific truth
is discerned and of the experience in which aesthetic
contemplation is enjoyed. And the two accounts are
in essentials the same. Yet, while the West is prepared to recognize the second set of experiences as
valid, it ignores the religious experience, or writes
it off as mere psychological subjectivism. Thus
what Radhakrishnan says in effect is this. 'If you
are prepared to concede the existence of a faculty,
Intuition, which discovers new truth in science and
mathematics, and is the vehicle of what you call
creative inspiration in art, what possible grounds
have you for denying its efficacy in the sphere of
religion? If the mind makes jumps in the apprehension of a new significance in painting and
music and of the hitherto unrealized implications
of propositions, may it not also jump to the apprehension of reality as spiritual? If it transcends the
subject-object relation in aesthetic contemplation,
so that the contemplator enters into the being of
that which excites him, why should it not do so
in religious ecstasy, so that the individual spirit becomes merged in the universal consciousness? You
cannot, in short, admit the efficacy of this faculty
in one sphere without admitting it in another;
the evidence suggests that, if applicable at all, it
is equally applicable in both. If you enquire where
that evidence is to be found, I must refer you to the
contemporary mystics of the East and the historic
mystics of the West. The absence of such evidence,
owing to the comparative atrophy of the spiritual

faculty in the contemporary West, is a misfortune; it is not a ground for denying that the evidence has ever existed. You have only to read the testimony of the great Christian mystics to convince yourself. And, finally, if you admit the efficacy of the faculty, you must admit the validity of its deliverances, and, in so doing, you will find that you have only put into the quasi-scientific terminology of modern psychology what the East in the accents of faith could always have told you.'

SUMMARY OF ACCOUNT OF INTUITION

So much being premised, we may summarize Radhakrishnan's account of intuition and of the part which it plays in religious experience as follows. First, intuition is a genuine revelation of truth and reality; in fact, intuitional activity is the primary, if not the sole, mode of our approach to the real. Secondly, intuition will be, therefore, the instrument of the philosopher, as well as the activity of the mystic, in so far as philosophy purports to be the study of the real.

Thirdly, intuition is direct, and gives immediate certitude; it is not a continuation of ratiocinative activity; it involves a jump to a new level of apprehension. No doubt it provides the raw material for logical reasoning—"We invent by intuition, though we prove by logic,"[1]—but the subsequent proof does nothing to increase the intuitive certitude. It only enables it to be communicated.

[1] *An Idealist View of Life*, p. 177.

Fourthly, there is not, however, any definite gap between intuitive and intellectual activity; intuition and intellect are not separate and distinct faculties. To suppose, as Bergson does, that they are, leads to the disabling conclusion that the intellect does not give us metaphysical truth, in which event no philosophy which asserts that it does not can be true. Intuitional knowledge is not so much non-rational as non-conceptual; it dispenses with the mediation of concepts not of reason. "Both intellect and intuition belong to the self," but "while the former involves a specialized part, the latter employs the whole self. The two are synthesized in the self, and their activities are interdependent."[1]

Fifthly, intuition is not to be confused with what is commonly called instinct, or with the libido of the psycho-analysts. Intuition succeeds and crowns discursive thought; instinctive activity in the history both of the race and of individuals precedes it. Continuous instinctive activity is that from which man has evolved; continuous intuitive activity that to which he may hope to aspire.

APPLICATION TO CONTEMPORARY PHILOSOPHY

In order to throw his position into relief, I have emphasized Radhakrishnan's insistence on the necessity of conceding to intuition in religious insight the function which is now generally conceded to it in aesthetic experience. But in a complete account we should have to extend its scope to include the

[1] *An Idealist View of Life,* p. 153.

philosophical as well as the religious approach to reality. Arguments were advanced earlier in the chapter[1] to suggest that, in so far as a whole is more than the sum of its parts, the 'more' is apprehended intuitionally. This, we pointed out, is true of all wholes which are really wholes; it is as true of our knowledge of a joke as it is of our knowledge of a personality. In so far, then, as reality is a whole—and Radhakrishnan holds that in an important sense it is—the knowledge of reality must also be intuitional.

Hence, Radhakrishnan concludes, philosophy which deals on purely intellectualist lines with abstract and purely logical problems can never achieve a grasp of reality. In proportion as its approach is exclusively intellectual, it will lose influence, and finally peter out in a bog of sterile abstraction: "It is a mistake to think that the only qualifications for elucidating truth in the sphere of philosophy are purely intellectual."[2] Yet it is a mistake which is, apparently, in Radhakrishnan's view, continuously made by the philosophers of the contemporary West. "If the philosophers to-day are not so influential as they used to be, it is to no small extent due to the fact that they are specializing in abstruse problems which are beyond the comprehension of the layman. They manipulate abstract concepts with the weapons of logical analysis. Philosophy which was once the pursuit of wisdom has become the possession

[1] See pp. 95–97.
[2] *An Idealist View of Life*, p. 182.

of a technique."[1] "The great systems of the past," he continues significantly, "had an adequate sense of the vastness of the universe and the mysteries of the soul."[1]

It is open to doubt whether in these strictures Radhakrishnan is entirely fair to modern Western philosophy. Macmurray's book, *Freedom in the Modern World*, and Bertrand Russell's series of books on what may be called applied philosophy, *Sceptical Essays*, *Marriage and Morals* and *The Conquest of Happiness*, represent a movement to restore the contact between philosophy and life, and to bring man's thought about the universe as a whole down from the clouds to its original place, which is the market-place.

[1] *An Idealist View of Life*, p. 182.

CHAPTER IV

THE UNIVERSE AS A SPIRITUAL UNITY

I. *Intuition and Intellect in Art*

CAN INTUITION BE VALIDATED?

The considerations advanced in the last two chapters entitle us, in Radhakrishnan's view, to accept on trust the testimony of intuition in regard to the universe, a testimony which affirms that it is a whole, that it is a unity, and that it is spiritual. It is now our business to see how far this testimony can be made acceptable to the speculative reason and conformable with its requirements. Strictly this demand for conformity should not be made. Intuition brings immediate certitude; the deliverances of the religious consciousness are, we are assured, sufficient guarantee of their own authenticity. We should not, then, seek for corroboratory justification. Nor, so far as our basic assurance is concerned, do we.

This basic assurance which the intuitive deliverances of the religious consciousness are said to give us is that the universe has value and that it is fundamentally good. The religious consciousness, it will be remembered, is conceived by Radhakrishnan as the response of the personality to the universe as a whole. He points out, further, that those who are not fully integrated beings are unable to make this response, simply because they are not themselves wholes.

GREAT ART THE RESPONSE OF THE WHOLE SPIRIT

This notion of integrated response—if I may be pardoned a digression on art at the beginning of a chapter on the universe—has an important bearing upon Radhakrishnan's views of art and literature. The greatest artists are, says Radhakrishnan, those who have responded with their *whole* beings to the world as a *whole*, and, so responding, they have insisted that it is good. This is why the greatest tragedies, *Hamlet*, or *Lear*, or the *Agamemnon* of Aeschylus, do not depress but, in spite of the suffering they portray, exalt and ennoble, assuring us of a fundamental decency in things.

The human spirit can, they tell us, rise superior to circumstance, and it can do this because it is continuous with a universal spirit which owns a reality greater than that of circumstance. The friendly and the spiritual underlies and conditions the alien and the brutal. So much the great artists, by virtue of their penetrative insight into the nature of things, have realised, and, embodying their vision in their art, they generate in their readers or audiences a serene assurance which is lacking from the work of the contemporary West.

Modern Western literature, like much of modern Western philosophy (see above, p. 109), is not the fruit of the response of the whole man to the universe as a whole, but of isolated human faculties, of intellect, of humour, of fancy or even concupiscence, to isolated aspects of the universe. Like science it analyses and takes to bits; like science it is the product of a highly developed intellectual technique; and it fails, as science fails, to give us information about the underlying realities of life. With all its capacity for observation and analysis, modern literature remains, even in the hands of its greatest masters, Shaw and Wells, incapable of prescribing for the ills it diagnoses. Analysing with the intellect instead of feeling with the spirit, its authors deal, and deal necessarily, with phenomena only, not with the spiritual realities which underlie them. Failing to penetrate to true causes, they fail equally to suggest adequate remedies. These strictures upon great writers are not, I cannot help thinking, justified. Shaw's *Back to Methuselah* contains at once a positive account of the nature of the universe and a constructive theory of conduct of the first order of originality, while Wells's *Outline of History*, to name one book among many, has done more to create a sense of the unity of the human race and a realization of the consequent need for world government, a need which, as we shall see,[1] Radhakrishnan himself endorses, than that of any other writer of our time. This is, however, not the place to pursue these observations.

The conclusion of Radhakrishnan's strictures on current Western literature brings us again to the position of the last chapter; it is only by religious

[1] See Ch. VII, pp. 234–240.

H

insight that we can sense the underlying reality of things, and, we now add, it is only those who have intuitively sensed reality as a whole who achieve the greatest results in art. But although it is not the function of reason to cognize reality, reason may legitimately be employed to give an account of the reality which insight discovers. To this account we must now turn our attention.

II. Is the Universe One or Two?

THE UNIVERSE DESCRIBED

The universe, says Radhakrishnan, is a spiritual unity. The real is an Absolute, pure, passionless, perfect, changeless and eternal. The cosmic process of change and evolution, the world we know, is not the Absolute but an aspect of it only. It is related to the Absolute in a very peculiar way. It is a realization or actualization of one of an infinite number of possibilities in which the Absolute might have chosen to realize itself, but the only one in which it did in fact realize itself. Freedom, as we sense it in ourselves, consists of the ability to choose or reject any one of a number of possibilities presented to us. Now the Absolute is free; it is also infinite; therefore it "has an infinite number of possibilities to choose from, which are all determined by its nature."[1]

Hence, "while the possible is determined by the nature of the Absolute, the actual is selected from

[1] *An Idealist View of Life*, p. 343.

out of the total amount of the possible by the free activity of the Absolute without any determination whatsoever. It could have created a world different in every detail from that which is actual. If one drama is enacted and other possible ones postponed, it is due to the freedom of the Absolute."[1]

The world as we know it, then, is not a *mere* appearance in the sense in which the Absolute alone is reality; it is a reality in which the possibility which is the Absolute actualized itself, when it might have chosen to actualize itself differently—might, and, since it has infinite time at its disposal, still may, "the creation of the world" being "an incident in the never-ending activity of the Absolute."[1]

OPPOSING VIEWS REJECTED

Into the reasons which Radhakrishnan gives for these assertions I do not propose to enter. They consist largely of a demonstration of the impossibility of any alternative conception of reality. Alternative conceptions are impossible because sooner or later they involve self-contradiction. Radhakrishnan demonstrates this conclusion with considerable force in relation to rival conceptions of reality which are prominently advocated in the contemporary philosophy of the West; the organic theory of Whitehead, which represents reality after the model of a *living* whole; the Holism of General Smuts, which represents it as a creative process of whole-making in time; the creative evolutionary

[1] *An Idealist View of Life*, p. 344.

hypothesis of Bergson; Professor Alexander's conception of reality as a process of emergence from a matrix of Space-Time; and the doctrine of the Italian Idealists that it is the activity of creative spirit. Many of these views are examined in detail in Radhakrishnan's early book, *The Reign of Religion in Contemporary Philosophy*, and attributed rather surprisingly to the unconscious influence of vestigial religious beliefs upon the minds of their authors.

I pass over this critical phase of the argument that I may come the more rapidly to two fundamental problems, which, if Radhakrishnan's view is right, immediately present themselves. His treatment of these problems is peculiarly relevant, since it affords a good example of that synthesis between Eastern and Western thought of which I spoke in the first chapter.

DIFFICULTIES

I. WHY SHOULD THE ABSOLUTE CREATE?

The first is, why should the Absolute actualize itself at all, or why, to adopt the more conventional language of Western theology, should God[1] create the world? And, further, waiving the question of motive, is it in any way compatible with known facts that He should have created it?

Taking the first question first, God being perfect

[1] The relation of God to the Absolute in Radhakrishnan's metaphysic will be considered in the next section of this chapter.

cannot, as Plato pointed out, change. For change is either for the better or for the worse. If God could change for the worse, He is not perfect, since He possesses the potentiality for deterioration; if for the better, it follows again that He is not perfect, since there is some good, that, namely, which He achieves by changing which He lacks. Now, creation implies change; it implies that one brings into being something that does not already exist, because, presumably, what *does* already exist is not completely satisfying. But a perfect being cannot feel need or desire and yet remain perfect. Now one creates, presumably, because one feels need and desire, the need to change what is, the desire for what is to be created. God, therefore, being *ex hypothesi* exempt from need and desire, could have no incentive to create.

2. PAIN, EVIL, ERROR AND MULTIPLICITY;
THE PROBLEM STATED

The difficulty raised by the second question is no less formidable. This world, it is obvious, is not perfect; it contains evil and pain. Either, then, we must say that God deliberately willed to produce something less good than Himself, or persuade ourselves that these things, evil and pain, are in some sense illusory. But if they are illusory, then the error I make in thinking them to be real—and not only in life do I find them to be real enough, but my philosophical views endorse my experience—is not illusory. There is no doubt that I *believe*

myself to suffer and *think* men do me evil. If I am
mistaken in so thinking owing to the illusoriness of
pain and evil, my mistake cannot itself be illusory.
Thus, if pain and evil are illusions, error is not. It
is real in just the same sense as God or the Absolute
is real.

Let us restate the difficulty in the somewhat
different form in which it presents itself, if we
substitute the logic of the Absolute for the benevo-
lence of a personal and omnipotent God. If reality
is a spiritual unity, a perfect and passionless Absolute,
then the world of many different things which we
certainly *seem* to experience is either truly a part
of the Absolute, real in the sense in which it is real,
or it is not. If it is, this manyness, and, we may add,
this imperfection, are real factors in the universe
which is not, therefore, a perfect unity. If it is not,
then two difficulties arise: first, they are in *some
sense* parts of or aspects of the Absolute, since the
Absolute comprises all that there is; hence it would
seem that the Absolute expresses itself in aspects or
manifestations which are less real than itself, that
it voluntarily abates, as it were, its own claim to
complete reality by the exfoliation of illusory aspects.
Secondly, there is no doubt that I *think* there are
many things in the world. But if there are not *really*
many things, then this error of mine in supposing
that there are is a real error. If it were unreal, it
would not be a mistake to suppose that there were
many things, and there would be many things.
Therefore the Absolute contains or comprises error,

not as an illusory principle, but as a real factor in itself.

These are difficulties which all views which assert the fundamental spiritual unity of the world must meet. If there is a reality behind the world of appearances, how do we account for the world of appearances?

ARE THE DIFFICULTIES INSOLUBLE?

These difficulties are, Radhakrishnan is inclined to suggest, insoluble. "As to why there is realization of this possibility, we can only say that it is much too difficult for us in the pit to know what is happening behind the screens. It is māyā, or a mystery which we have to accept reverently."[1] And in *The Hindu View of Life* he tells us that "the history of philosophy in India as well as Europe has been one long illustration of the inability of the human mind to solve the relation of God to the world. The greatest thinkers are those who admit the mystery and comfort themselves by the idea that the human mind is not omniscient."[2]

That the difficulties are incapable of solution on Monist lines is indeed, in the view of many, including the present writer, a plain fact, and it is this fact which, they hold, necessitates the inclusion in the universe of some principle or factor to break up the unity and engender the world of plurality, even if plurality be held to be only an appearance.

[1] *An Idealist View of Life*, p. 344.
[2] *The Hindu View of Life*, pp. 67, 68.

RADHAKRISHNAN ON EVIL

To take the second problem first, the existence of some principle other than the spiritual unity which Radhakrishnan postulates as ultimate reality, is, those of us who are pluralists would hold, required from the point of view of ethics to account for the existence of pain and evil. The failure to provide an adequate treatment of these undoubted facts of experience is indeed, in my opinion, a definite weakness in Radhakrishnan's philosophy. His view seems to be that the principles of Karma and rebirth[1] enable us to explain the nature and understand the function of evil, without compelling us to include it as a real feature in the spiritual unity which is reality. These "principles," he says, "suggest to us that the value of the world is not in any way affected by the actuality of evil, error and ugliness."[2] This view will be further developed in the next chapter where Radhakrishnan's ethical philosophy will be considered as a whole.

THE NEED FOR A FURTHER PRINCIPLE

For the present I content myself with the remark that this deficiency in the treatment of pain and evil is in no way peculiar to Radhakrishnan's philosophy; it is one which his view exhibits in common with that of all Monists. It is because we demand a more substantial and realistic treatment

[1] See next chapter, pp. 172–174 and 182–190.
[2] *An Idealist View of Life*, p. 333.

that many of us are driven to embrace pluralist views. For it is not the case, as Radhakrishnan sometimes seems to suggest, that Monism is the only *possible* view open to a human mind which really seeks to understand the nature of the universe. Many great thinkers, Plato and Aristotle for example, in the past, William James and Bertrand Russell in our own times, have abjured the view that the world is a unity through and through, and invoked principles ranging from Plato's τὸ μὴ ὄν[1] to Russell's neutral particulars to break up the unity and to dilute the alleged homogeneity of reality, seeking by this means to give some account of what Plato would call the *semi-reality* of the familiar world of daily experience. Nor is Radhakrishnan himself indifferent to the attraction of this mode of interpretation. For—that I may come at last to his own contribution to the problem we are considering—he too, in spite of his official Monism, has paid a tribute to the seductions of a further principle.

ŚAṀKARA'S VIEW

In his celebrated work on *Indian Philosophy* Radhakrishnan describes the view of the creation advanced by the Hindu philosopher Śaṁkara. Śaṁkara conceives of God after the likeness of an artist finding an outlet for his overflowing energy and vitality in creation. The thing created expresses

[1] "Plato held that the goodness of God was made somewhat ineffective by the intractableness of nature, which He tried in vain to control."—*The Hindu View of Life*, p. 68.

and canalizes the overflow. The theory has its roots in antiquity, "The great symbol of the sun which is used in Hindu thought . . . signifies the generous self-giving and ecstasy of the Absolute, which overflows and gives itself freely and generously to all. . . . The Indian figure of līlā makes the creation of the universe an act of playfulness. Play is generally the expression of the ideal possibilities. It is its own end and its own continuous reward."[1] "The perfection of God overflows into the world. The world is the outflow of the surplus energies of God, the supreme artist."[2] So far so good; the simile is a happy one, and supplies a motive for God's creation without raising the difficulty of attributing to Him desire or need. God creates not because of His lack but because of His abundance, an abundance which is so great that it cannot contain itself.

But, if we are to take the artist analogy seriously, we cannot overlook the fact that the artist uses a medium. He cannot express himself *in vacuo*; he requires paint and canvas, stone and sound. And of necessity. Were there no medium, the artist would not and could not create; he would merely *be*. Now I have heard Radhakrishnan in the course of a lecture emphasize this very necessity, and maintain that the necessity is absolute. The conclusion is plain. If God's creation is to be conceived after the manner of the artist's, then there must be a medium besides God in which He expresses Himself.

[1] *An Idealist View of Life*, p. 344.
[2] *The Hindu View of Life*, p. 69.

Grant the medium, and the difficulties of Monism are in a fair way to being solved. But how reconcile the medium itself with Monism? I do not know. I am content to mention this ingenious notion which Radhakrishnan has adopted from Śaṁkara, the notion of God as artist, and leave to him the task of reconciling it with the Monism he so eloquently maintains. I suspect that the reconciliation would represent both God and the world—the artist and the medium—as but two sides of a temporary cosmic process, which is itself an expression of an underlying Absolute. It is to the nature of this Absolute that I now turn.

III. God and The Absolute

THE DEMANDS OF REASON AND THE MESSAGE OF EXPERIENCE

I come now to the first problem raised by Radhakrishnan's metaphysics, the problem of God's nature with special reference to the surprising fact of His creation of the world.

Radhakrishnan's treatment of this question is characteristic and original. The view of the universe as a single, spiritual Absolute is reached by the operations of the speculative reason. It is as if Radhakrishnan, sitting quietly in his study, had put to himself the question, "What sort of universe must this be in order that the facts of life and experience may be as they are?" and answered, "It must be a spiritual Absolute!" The conclusion was not, that is to say, revealed to him in a blinding flash of *intuitive* experience, nor did he take into account *experiences* reported by others. He worked the thing out by sheer process of reasoning, exactly as if it were a problem in mathematics.

In addition to those who have sought knowledge by means of the intellect, the history of philosophy bears witness to a long line of thinkers who have insisted that the proper approach to reality was that of experiment and observation. In addition to the type of mind which has proclaimed the demand of the speculative reason that the universe must be X, there is the type which has insisted that as a matter of plain experience it is Y. In addition to mathematics, in fact, there is physical science. The distinction is between *a priori* and empirical knowledge, between that which reason demands and that which experience reveals, and the record of philosophical speculation shows that either is ignored at our peril. Hence, having reached the Absolute by *a priori* methods, Radhakrishnan proceeds to correct, or rather to supplement, his view by a resort to experience. Direct spiritual experience is, we have agreed, the foundation of religion. It is the raw material which the theologians and philosophers seek to rationalize. To the reports of this experience we have so far in this chapter paid scant attention.

Yet, in Radhakrishnan's view, their reading is plain enough. In addition to the revealing of the Absolute, they point also to the existence of a personal God deeply concerned in the affairs of the world, loving, judging and redeeming mankind, a God who, while immeasurably transcending, is also immanent in us, is, in fact, the very core and centre of our beings. And the problem is to square the existence of this personal God with the kind of Absolute that the speculative reason and religious experience on occasion demand. The reasoning employed is subtle, and I propose to indicate the main steps of the argument in Radhakrishnan's own words.

REASON DEMANDS THE ABSOLUTE; EXPERIENCE GOD

First, for various reasons mainly of a critical and negative order, we must regard this world as an aspect of or an emanation from a creative spirit: "The inadequacy of naturalism shows that the world process with its order and creativity requires for its explanation a creative power. For, however far we may travel backwards in space or time, we cannot jump out of space-time, and we cannot account for space-time structure. The rationality of the universe suggests that the creative power is mind or spirit."[1]

Secondly, we are entitled to trust our reason in this matter, since our reason is itself part of reality. "Our logical concepts . . . are not forms superinduced on reality, but are determinate forms of reality itself."[2]

But, thirdly, the bare affirmation of a spiritual

[1] *An Idealist View of Life*, p. 331.
[2] Ibid., p. 333.

reality which is also creative does not provide for certain plain facts of experience, the facts, namely, of religious experience and of the moral consciousness. "God as the universal mind working with a conscious design, who is at once the beginning of the world, the author of its order, the principal of its progress and the goal of its evolution, is not the God of religion unless we take into account the facts of religious consciousness.[1] It is "our moral life," which "tells us that God is not only the goal but the spring and sustainer of moral effort, our spiritual experience," which "reveals to us the fact of the supreme all-comprehensive one."[1] In Radhakrishnan's striking phrase, in mystical experience "our eyes are opened, and they all declare the presence of the one Supreme. The universe seems to be alive with spirit, aglow with fire, burning with light."[2]

Fourthly, we can trust our spiritual intuition and mystical experience since of "our intuitive apprehensions" also we may say that they "are not forms superinduced on reality, but are determinate forms of reality itself."[3]

THE ANTINOMY; GOD AND THE ABSOLUTE

Here, then, we seem to have two conflicting demands: the demand of the speculative reason and abstract mysticism for an all-embracing spiritual Absolute, impersonal, passionless and aloof, and the

---

[1] *An Idealist View of Life*, p. 333.
[2] Ibid., p. 109.   [3] Ibid., p. 333.

demand of the mass of religious experience for a personal God, interested, rejoicing and suffering. That the demands are at first sight incompatible is sufficiently clear. It is, for example, a postulate of the mystical experience that the spirit of the mystic merges at least temporarily with that of the supreme. This postulate Radhakrishnan endorses. Yet how, it may be asked, can that which is in time coalesce with that which is timeless; or how can that which is imperfect fuse with and form part of the perfect without infecting the perfect with its own imperfection?

Again, since the Absolute is timeless, it cannot admit of change. Yet there is a continuing strain of thought in philosophy and of testimony in theology which insists that God does change, suffering and rejoicing with mankind and growing in fullness of being with the development of the human spirit. This last conception is particularly prevalent in the contemporary West. Alexander's metaphysic conceives of God as continuously evolving, emerging afresh as a *potential* level of development each time a new actual level is realized, while Italian Idealism equates the Absolute life of the universe with the history of the human spirit. What relation have these views of deity, which generated within the matrix of the Western concept of evolution insist on change as a fundamental feature of the real, with the changeless Absolute of Oriental thought? This contradiction—the contradiction between reality as an emotionless Absolute and reality as personal God—

is, in Radhakrishnan's view, the supreme problem of theology.

GOD AND THE ABSOLUTE; SUGGESTED SOLUTION

"The great problem of the philosophy of religion has been the reconciliation of the character of the Absolute as in a sense eternally complete with the character of God as a self-determining principle manifested in a temporal development which includes nature and man."[1]

The hint of Radhakrishnan's solution is to be found in the attitude, already sketched in Chapter II, to religious conceptions as symbolic representations of a reality which underlies them. Just as the atom is a symbol of an unknown physical reality, so God is a symbol of an unknown spiritual reality. The concept of God, in a word, is like the solar-system picture of the atom; we contrive for ourselves the nearest thing our minds can manage to a reality which inevitably transcends their limitations. "The idea of God" in fact "is an interpretation of experience."[2] It is not a direct revelation of an objectively real individual. Thus all religion is from its very nature symbolic: "The monotheists are quite certain that the gods of the polytheists are symbolic if not mythological presentations of the true God; but they are loth to admit that their own God is at bottom a symbol."[3] Yet this, in Radhakrishnan's view, is precisely what He is, "a

---

[1] *An Idealist View of Life*, p. 343.
[2] Ibid., p. 86.   [3] Ibid., p. 109.

symbol in which religion cognizes the Absolute."[1]
On these lines we approach the solution which
Radhakrishnan offers for the problem posed above,
a solution which insists that God and the Absolute
are not two disparate entities, but that God is the
way in which the Absolute appears to and is known
by us. God is thus "the Absolute from the human
end."[2]

The Absolute is, as we have seen, at once the sum
and the source of limitless possibilities. One of the
possibilities has become actualized, and to this
actualized possibility of itself the Absolute stands
in a special relation. It is in this relation, the special
relation in which it stands to the actually existing
fact of the world, that the Absolute appears as God,
a being guiding and loving the world, conscious of
its general plan and direction even before it was
actualized in space-time, and deeply concerned to
see that the plan should be realized. This is not to
say that the symbol God is a *mere* figment of our
minds, since, as we have seen in Chapter II, the
deliverances of our minds themselves reflect the
structure of reality.

A twofold relatedness of God is thus envisaged.
First, from the side of man, God is the mode under
which man represents to himself his experience of
the Absolute. God is a symbol of reality, which is
nevertheless a real symbol. Secondly, from the side
of reality, God is an aspect of the Absolute in its

[1] *An Idealist View of Life*, p. 109.
[2] Ibid., p. 344.

I

relation to that particular one of its infinite possibilities which has been actualized.

CHANGELESSNESS AND CHANGE

Before I proceed to describe the main features of Radhakrishnan's conception of God, I propose very briefly to consider the significance of this solution. The suggestion which Radhakrishnan makes is in effect a bridge between the traditional religious thought of the East and the religious experience of the West interpreted in terms of the contemporary scientific concepts of the West.

It has been a postulate of most religious views of the universe that at the heart of things there is something which is changeless and perfect. This conclusion is the final outcome of Plato's philosophy; it is reached and stated in a different form by Hegel; it is the presupposition of the ontological proof for God's existence; it is the distinguishing declaration of the religious testimony of the East. Changelessness and permanence, it is urged, there must be in the universe, else we should have no criterion whereby to recognize the changing. Time can have no meaning in a world in which there is only time. Perfection, again, there must be; otherwise we should have no standard whereby to recognize imperfection. Such are the axioms upon which the traditional Eastern view rests.

But of recent years, under the influence of science, there has arisen in the West a demand for a different kind of reality. This demand is bound up with the discovery and teaching of evolution, with the resultant recognition of the activity of life as a dynamic, changing principle, and the acceptance of human life as its most eminent expression. Spirit, and the values which express spirit, must, it is urged as a corollary, change and develop as life changes and develops; moreover, spiritual values must in the last resort be of the same nature as, and therefore capable of union with, the ideal development of that most eminent and admired expression of life, the human spirit. Value, in fact, is only an expression, albeit an idealized one, of the human spirit. It is the product of creative thinking not discovered but projected by the free self-determining activity of mind, which is the author at once of its world and of itself. For Croce and Gentile nothing is real but Spirit, and Spirit is naught but the process without beginning and without end of its own absolute self-creation. Nothing, therefore, is but thinking makes it so in the act of its own self-formation. Spirit or mind is thus the author of all forms, degrees, grades or stages of being, and, being conceived on the model of self-consciousness, must posit itself as object and concurrently as subject, while it still remains one with itself. Value, then, in so far as it is apprehended as an object, is merely the postulation by mind as subject of mind as object. Notable expressions of this doctrine are Croce's mystery of the infinite progress and infinite perfectibility of man, and Professor Alexander's conception of deity as a perpetually unrealized quality of the evolutionary process of which we ourselves form part.

RADHAKRISHNAN'S CONCESSION TO BOTH VIEWS

It is these two demands, the demand that reality should be changeless, the demand that it should be changing, that Radhakrishnan's view seeks to reconcile, and the reconciliation is effected by means of the ingenious use of an argument by analogy from modern science.

'Science, physicists are increasingly agreed, does not,' says Radhakrishnan in effect, 'give us direct knowledge of reality. It only represents reality to us under symbolic forms. Very well, then, religious insight does the same. While man may achieve a direct intuitive view of the real, he can represent his vision to his fellows only under symbolic forms. The particular form of symbolism used will be relative to and determined by the knowledge and culture of the age. And the symbolic conception which happens to be appropriate to the spirit of this age is that of a changing, evolving God, who is also the changing, evolving spirit in man'. What are the attributes of God so conceived?

ATTRIBUTES OF GOD

In the first place, God, not God who is the Absolute, but God who is the personal guide and supervisor of the world, is organic with the world. He participates, therefore, in time and change. He evolves as the world evolves; He may even be regarded as a sharer in its imperfection.

"Struggle and growth are real in the life of God. Time is the essential form of the cosmic process, including the moral life, and it has a meaning for God also. Life eternal, which carries us beyond the limit of temporal growth, may take us to the Absolute, but God is essentially bound up with the life in time."[1]

GOD NOT MERELY THE SPIRIT IN MAN

This is to introduce God into the world with a vengeance. Is He, one is tempted to ask, on this basis, anything but a grand name for the changing and evolving spirit of man? Radhakrishnan answers first, that, whatever else He may or may not be, He *is* assuredly the spirit in man. He is, in fact, the very core and essence of our being. This conclusion is reached by two different routes. First, in the light of the considerations which Monism stresses, we are assured of the organic unity of the world. The world, we have seen, is a single all-embracing spirit, and any apparent separateness between, any apparent plurality of its aspects is not a real separateness, a real plurality. Just as Bradley conceived of the Absolute as that which, moving obscurely in everything, becomes conscious of itself in man, so Radhakrishnan sees the universal spirit achieving in man a consciousness of its own fundamental unity. Man, in other words, becomes

[1] *An Idealist View of Life*, p. 338.

conscious of the fact that there is God and that his spirit is one with God. But in becoming conscious of the fact that there is God—and herein is the gist of the answer—he is conscious also that the God is not *merely* the spirit in himself and his fellows, but is a transcendent reality with which his spirit is continuous. The appeal here is to the testimony of direct experience; and it is of just this fact of continuity with a "more" that the teaching of mystical experience, we are told, assures us. "The consubstantiality of the spirit in man and God is the conviction fundamental to all spiritual wisdom. It is not a matter of inference only. In the spiritual experience itself the barriers between the self and the ultimate reality drop away."[1] And again, "In mystic states we become one with the Absolute and we become aware of our oneness."[2] Thus reason and experience both point in the same direction to establish the fact of our fundamental unity with God.

IS OUR INDIVIDUALITY LOST IN GOD?

The doctrine has an important bearing upon ethics. Much has been written upon the subject of the nature and validity of the mystical state. Is the mystical experience a projection of the whimsies of our unconscious mind upon the empty canvas of a mindless universe, or is it the medium of the soul's intercourse with God? Are the utterances of the

[1] *An Idealist View of Life*, p. 103.
[2] Ibid., p. 105.

mystics the babblings of men beside themselves with fasting and solitude, or do they truly report the nature of the real world? To these questions Radhakrishnan, as we have seen, replies unequivocally that the religious experience has just as good a claim to give information about the nature of the real as science or art, perception or common sense—it has, indeed, if the argument of the last chapter can be accepted, a better claim—and the clearest of the windows of the religious consciousness through which men look out upon the real world is the faculty of the mystic.

But, assuming that we are prepared to accept Radhakrishnan's estimate of mysticism, other questions arise. Does the mystical experience involve a merging of the individual soul in a reality that transcends it? If so, does it not mean the obliteration of individuality? We are attached to our individualities in the West and apt to regard the human personality as the highest expression of itself, the highest *spiritual* expression, that life has hitherto succeeded in evolving. Under the influence of this attitude we do not regard the extinction of individuality with equanimity. Yet Radhakrishnan, as we have seen, endorses the claim of the Christian mystics that in mystical experience the self is fused with its object. Finally, whether the mystical experience does or does not involve submergence of the individual in the infinite, can it in any event be regarded as accessible to the ordinary man? Is it not rather a special vocation for unusually gifted human beings?

GOD AS THE ESSENCE OF MAN

Upon the answers to these questions the doctrine of God as the inmost essence of the human spirit has an important bearing. For, if God is the core of our being, to become one with God is nothing less than to realize ourselves. To realize God in the self is not, then, to destroy individuality but to affirm it.

"There is," says Radhakrishnan, "in the self of man, at the very centre of his being, something deeper than the intellect, which is akin to the Supreme."[1]

It follows that the way of life which reveals the vision of the supreme is also a way of life which realizes the self. Thus the problem constituted by the supposed loss of individuality in union with God is seen to be unreal. "In the moment of its highest insight the self becomes aware not only of its own existence but of the existence of an omnipotent spirit of which it is, as it were, a focussing."[1]

AFFINITY WITH PLATONISM

Once again we catch the Platonic strain in Radhakrishnan's thought. The soul of man, says Plato, existed once as pure spirit in a heavenly place, where it enjoyed a continuous and untrammelled contemplation of the Forms. It is incarnated in matter, or, to use Platonic language, it is mixed with "not being," and so enters the world of

[1] *An Idealist View of Life*, p. 103.

"becoming". Here it is haunted by the memory of the beauty and goodness it has known in its pure state before association with an alien material had blurred its vision. And the reason for the excitement which beauty rouses in us is that it reminds the soul, tantalizingly and evanescently, it may be, but none the less unmistakably, of what it has known but has forgotten. Ultimately the soul will shed the trappings of the distorting alien material in which it is now encased, and achieve again a pure untrammelled vision of the Forms. So Plato. . . . "If in spite of the identity of kinship between the soul and God the latter appears so far away, it is because the soul is immersed in what is alien to it, and finds it difficult to get at self-knowledge. Having drunk of the waters of Lethe . . . man has forgotten his heavenly origin. He is an exile from heaven, clothed in what seems an alien garment of flesh."[1] So Radhakrishnan. . . .

And for him, as for Plato, the object of learning and discipline, the ultimate 'good' of ethics and the end of man is to span the gulf that separates man from the real world, to overcome the barrier that intervenes by stripping away the "alien garment of flesh." But whereas, for Plato, the ultimate state is one of *knowing*, for Radhakrishnan it is one of *becoming* reality. And, in becoming reality, one becomes oneself; for reality, the spirit of God, is also, as we have seen, the essence of the spirit of man.

For Radhakrishnan, then, as for Plato, the process

[1] *An Idealist View of Life*, p. 111.

of the self's development is a process of stripping away unessential elements that separate it from being and hinder the realization of its true nature.

DUALISM AGAIN?

And if we press for an account of the alien investiture of flesh, ask whence come the waters of Lethe, and enquire how the soul of man became incarnated in what is other than itself, Radhakrishnan is no more ready than is Plato with a satisfactory answer. Just as it forced itself upon us, when we were asked to think of God's overflowing into a medium other than Himself, so the need for a further principle, a material substance, a blank, featureless medium, an obstructive, intractable environment, call it what you will, seems inescapable. Something, it appears, obstructs man's vision of God which is also his realization of himself. He falls below the full level of reality, in virtue of something that shuts him off from reality. What account are we to give of that something? Inevitably the question forces itself upon the mind of the confirmed dualist. But it cannot be pursued here without committing the author to embarking upon a general criticism of the monistic metaphysic which underlies this whole way of thought. I have attempted such a criticism elsewhere, and it would be obviously out of place to raise it here.[1]

If we waive this point, the lines upon which Radhakrishnan seeks to meet the criticism sometimes

[1] See my *Matter, Life and Value*, Ch. II.

levelled against the mystic experience that, in so far as it merges the individual in God, it destroys his individuality, should, in the light of the foregoing, be clear enough. Religious experience, in its most developed form, which is mystical experience, does not destroy individuality; it enhances it; and it does this because, in uniting the individual with God, it unites him with his true self. To the further question, 'Is this experience possible or, indeed, suitable for all men?' Radhakrishnan answers emphatically that it is. The consideration of this answer belongs, however, to the next chapter.

Two further conceptions which logically follow from Radhakrishnan's view of deity must be mentioned.

GOD'S DEMAND FOR HELP

If God changes and struggles with the changing and struggling world, if God is also the spirit in us, then, it is obvious, He has a right to demand our help in His struggle, if only because in helping God we are also helping ourselves to realize more fully our own true nature: "He expects us to recognize and respond to His call and co-operate with Him. . . . Our sin consists in distrusting God, in refusing to recognize His purpose and respond to His demand. Our virtue consists in assimilating the divine content and participating in His purpose."[1]

And the help which we are asked to give is not for the perpetuation of an endless process, but for

[1] *An Idealist View of Life*, p. 335.

the attainment of a definite goal. Unlike the modern philosophies of creative evolution which regard the cosmic process as an endless perfecting of the human spirit, the goal indefinitely receding as it is continually approached, Radhakrishnan conceives a definite state of fulfilment and fruition as the goal of the world's travail.

THE END AS UNITY

It is a state marked by the unification of the temporarily separated aspects of the spiritual structure which is reality. It is, in the first place, a unification in the sense that the human spirit overcomes the barriers which, in separating it from God, separate it also from its own self-realization. The spirit becomes God and, in so doing, becomes itself. When this consummation is reached, there is a complete identity between God and the world, the alien garment of matter, the flesh which now separates them being transcended. "God, though immanent, is not identical with the world until the very end. Throughout the process there is an unrealized residuum in God, but it vanishes when we reach the end."[1]

In the second place, there is unification in the sense that God Himself now recedes into and loses Himself in the Absolute. For God is in an important sense a creation of man. He is, it will be remembered, "the Absolute from the human end." But, if there is no longer humanity, but only God in whom the

[1] *An Idealist View of Life*, p. 340.

human spirit is completely realized, there is no 'human end' in relation to which God may be said to exist. "The world," we are told, "is as indispensable to God as God is to the world."[1] But, if the world has become God, if there is no longer any residuum of world which is left over outside God, then the necessity for both God and the world vanishes and both sink back into the all-embracing Absolute being.

If we may have recourse to a metaphor, let us think of the Absolute as an infinite sea of being. The finite mind, unable to grasp this infinity as a whole, concentrates upon the only aspect which it can comprehend, and calls into existence by the concentration of its attention upon this aspect a vortex or whorl in the sea. This vortex is God. At the end of the cosmic process the human mind itself sinks into and is absorbed by the vortex, and, owning no longer any title to being except that which is conferred upon it by its participation in the vortex, is no longer enabled, as it is enabled now, by virtue of the needs and limitations of its separated and partial comprehension, to call the vortex into existence. The vortex accordingly slips back into the sea, being transcended by it, just as it has itself transcended the knowing mind of man. Thus by the very act of eliminating that which now separates us from God, we eliminate also the distinction which appears to separate God from Absolute reality.

[1] *An Idealist View of Life*, p. 344.

EASTERN AND WESTERN THOUGHT FUSED

The whole conception bears witness to that incorporation of Western ideas within an Eastern framework, which is so pronounced a characteristic of Radhakrishnan's thought. The affirmation of an unchangeable reality and of individuality as a temporary phenomenon ultimately to be transcended as that reality is reached by the cosmic process, the conviction that the real is in us here and now and that it is only the veils of illusion that hide it from us and separate us from it, all these conceptions, it is obvious, come from the East. The recognition of change as also a reality, of the world process which we know as evolution as a real process, of the end as not pre-formed in the process but as real novelty existing in a real future, a novelty, moreover, which may even fail of achievement, all these elements derive from the thought of the West.

Urging that "the process of the world is not a mere unfolding of what is contained in the beginning,"[1] that the final end is not present at the outset, Radhakrishnan answers those who would deny the reality of novelty and change. Insisting that God is not something evolved by the process of cosmic change, that He is separate from it, transcending it in His aspect as Absolute, even if He is also immanent in it in His aspect of evolving spirit, Radhakrishnan invokes the traditional view of the East in opposition to theories of the Alexander or

[1] *An Idealist View of Life*, p. 339.

Bergson type which regard the universe as exhaustively analysable in terms of evolutionary concepts. Taken as a whole the system is, indeed, an admirably ingenious attempt to reconcile the claims of the two opposed and apparently irreconcilable concepts of change and eternity.

To the conflict between these two principles the history of philosophy bears constant witness. They are the two poles between which the pendulum of philosophical thought swings. The East has on the whole stressed the concept of permanence and the illusoriness of change; the West, under the influence of evolutionary theory, has chosen rather to interpret the universe in terms of a changing flux. Nowhere in the universe, it has been urged, is there anything permanent and stable from which the flux derives or to which it moves. Moreover, under the influence of the material progress of the last hundred years, man, elated by his victories over matter, has tended to identify the flux with the essence of his own nature, conceiving not only Utopia but reality on the plane of the infinite perfectibility of the human spirit.

THE RENAISSANCE OF VALUE

Of recent years there has been a reaction against this point of view, and the revival of philosophies of value suggests the need of the human soul for an element of permanence and perfection. These later philosophies testify to the recognition of the need for a non-human object to satisfy the hunger for perfection. Humanity, it is felt, cannot ever become an adequate object of man's worship; yet something there must be which can be worshipped without reserve. To identify the human spirit with reality is to deprive the universe both of splendour and of awe, and in so depriving it to rob the human spirit which aspires to it of the very greatness with which it is designed to invest it by reason of the fact that it can aspire.

It is difficult to avoid the conclusion that a philosophy which affirms only the changing and evolving spirit of man, even if that spirit be identified, as Radhakrishnan identifies it, with God, is a narrow and trivial view, which ignores the plain intimations of the religious consciousness and thus does violence to our deepest although least articulate convictions.

SUMMARY OF METAPHYSICAL VIEW

Radhakrishnan's philosophy escapes this charge of triviality. Making full allowance for the changing and developing spirit in man, and by his doctrine of a developing God who is organic with the world accepting this spirit as a true aspect of reality, Radhakrishnan nevertheless affirms the permanence, the perfection and the unity of the reality which underlies it. Moreover, he envisages an end to the process of evolution when the changing elements have reached a point at which, transcending the need for further change, they can be reabsorbed in the unity from which they sprang, man into God and God into the Absolute. The view is not in some respects unlike that which Shaw has suggested in *Back to Methuselah*.

AFFINITY WITH SHAW'S VIEW

Life for Shaw is incarnate in matter. The consequence of this incarnation is to generate individuality by separating from each other life's infinite currents, each current of life being, as it were, isolated from the main stream (Radhakrishnan's God) by the barrier of the material medium. The object of evolution is so to develop the latent powers of life that the individual currents are to an ever diminishing extent limited by the material medium and are ultimately enabled to transcend it altogether. The Ancients in the last play of the Pentateuch have already achieved an almost complete emancipation from bodily needs and limitations. They no longer sleep or eat or talk. They have achieved such power over the body that they are enabled to change their physical structure at will. Barring accidents they can live indefinitely, but, so long as the body continues to exist as an accompaniment of life, their lives are subject to any hazard that may destroy the body. Meantime they are occupied in thinking. The vast tracts of their prodigious lives are, indeed, devoted entirely to that study of reality which in its initial stages in logic, mathematics, and science we to-day call thought. All the toys of men's past—images and pictures, love, romance and adventure—have one by one been discarded, and nothing remains interesting except thinking. The body is the last toy to be

K

given up, and, when that final emancipation has been achieved, there will be no people but only thought, and life will end as a whirlpool of pure intelligence, which began as a whirlpool in pure force. The object of evolution, then, as Shaw conceives it, is the attainment by life of a state of continuous and untrammelled thinking undisturbed by the solicitations of the body, that outworn heritage of man's past. Substitute "being" for "thinking" and for the immutable entities which the Ancients contemplate the Absolute reality into which the spirit merges; substitute for Shaw's Life Force the developing, changing God, who is himself but an aspect of the Absolute, and the two conceptions are in essentials the same. And their common merit is that, while making full allowance for the fact of change, they succeed in accommodating it within a world which is in the last resort a changeless unity,

CHAPTER V

WAY OF LIFE

I. Ethics and Religion

"Hinduism is more a way of life than a form of thought. While it gives absolute liberty in the world of thought, it enjoins a strict code of practice."[1] "Hinduism insists not on religious conformity but on a spiritual and ethical outlook in life."[1] These two quotations from *The Hindu View of Life* emphasize two points: the first, the wide toleration which Hinduism permits in the realm of belief, the second, the strict way of life which it prescribes in that of conduct. This broadness in believing and narrowness in behaving are two sides of the same coin; the one is the necessary obverse of the other. Together they enable and entitle Radhakrishnan to define Hinduism as "not a sect but a fellowship of all who accept the law of right and earnestly seek for the truth."[1] Radhakrishnan comes forward as the sponsor of both attitudes, the tolerance of belief, the strictness of practice. With the former we shall be concerned in Chapter VII; the latter, the Hindu way of life, so persuasively advocated by the author, will form part of the subject of this one.

[1] *The Hindu View of Life*, p. 77.

THE OBJECTIVE OF CONDUCT

Ethics cannot, it is obvious, on such a view as that outlined in the last chapter, be divorced from religion. Hinduism emphasizes the omnipresent reality of the spirit; all religions are, therefore, of value in its eyes, in so far as they are exercises and disciplines of the spirit. Thus each man is exhorted to find his own salvation by the light of his own creed. Hinduism, we are told, "does not believe in any statutory methods of salvation."[1] But in affirming that creed is not essential, we are at the same time affirming that conduct is. And conduct is essential not because it is a thing isolated from religion, but because the eternal verities, or as Radhakrishnan would put it, the realization of God, must be actively pursued in the day to day round of our ordinary avocations. The convenient maxim "to mix religion and business is to spoil two good things," so justly admired by the pious money-makers of the Victorian Age, has no countenance from Hinduism. We must live rightly and do our duty for its own sake, it is true; but also because, in so living and acting, we purify and refine the spirit and bring nearer the actualization of the divine which potentially informs it. Thus the knowledge of God, or rather the realization of the God in us, is the end of conduct, and ethics is the practice of religion.

Spiritual experience, as we saw in Chapter II,

[1] *The Hindu View of Life*, p. 50.

is at once the basis and the starting-point of religion. It is also its end; and in saying that it is the end of religion, we may say also that to achieve it is the object of living. If we use the word mysticism in its widest sense to denote the enjoyment of spiritual experience, we may say that mysticism is the end of life. Very well, then, it is our business so to live that we may enjoy mystical experience more fully, more intensely and more continuously. The objective of conduct may thus be defined as a continuous "discipline of human nature leading to a realization of the spiritual,"[1] a way of life which Radhakrishnan expressly defines as "mysticism."

THE RELIGIOUS WAY OF LIFE. WHAT IT INVOLVES

The religious life is nothing but a "spiritual certainty offering us strength and solace in the hour of need and sorrow. It is the conviction that love and justice are at the heart of the universe, that the spirit which gave rise to man will further his perfection."[2] So Radhakrishnan in the volume entitled *The Religion we Need* which he contributed to the series of *Affirmations* published by Sir Ernest Benn, the aim of which was stated to be to determine the place of God in the modern world. But, we are told, "we cannot reach this ideal of the religious life without deep meditation and strenuous self-discipline."[3] That this ideal *can* be achieved is the

[1] *Indian Philosophy*, Vol. I, p. 41.
[2] *The Religion we Need*, p. 27.
[3] Ibid., p. 28.

continuous teaching of Indian philosophy. It is because of this conviction that Indian philosophy has been so predominantly concerned with psychology. In the Introduction to his *Indian Philosophy*, a work which is likely to become a classic, Radhakrishnan emphasizes this characteristic and the reason for it: "Indian psychology realized the value of concentration and looked upon it as the means for the perception of the truth. It believed that there were no ranges of life or mind which could not be reached by a methodical training of will and knowledge."[1] To discipline the will to concentration, to train the soul to meditation, these are the objects of conduct! The bearing of these quotations is clear. The certainty of God, which is the essence or at any rate the foundation of the religious life, cannot be achieved except we follow a certain way of daily life. In order to think rightly, in order, in fact, to know the truth, we must live rightly.

ETHICS NOT SEPARABLE FROM RELIGION

Thus the ultimate explanation of right conduct, an explanation which is at once its rationale and its justification, is to be found not in itself but in something beyond itself. It is for this reason that systems of morals which rest upon no religious basis are found in practice to be inefficacious. The Roman Stoics for years protested against the gladiatorial games in the name of abstract humanity; yet it was left for a Christian, a certain monk, Telemachus,

[1] *Indian Philosophy*, Vol. I, p. 28.

who was almost certainly not a cultivated humanist, to leap into the arena and seal with his blood a protest which there was no need to repeat, for the protest was instantaneously successful. From that moment the games ceased. "No amount of earnest ethical exhortation can take the place of religion,"[1] Radhakrishnan concludes. Every word that he writes on ethical questions presupposes this intimate relation between ethics and religion, presupposes, indeed, as its basic assumption, the spiritual view of the universe, the spiritual nature of man and the concept of God as indwelling in man, which were sketched in the last chapter. If this assumption be not granted, the ethical philosophy which we shall outline in this one is without foundation.

AN OBJECTION. IS THE WORLD REAL?

The reference to metaphysics raises an inevitable objection. Given the metaphysical foundation laid in the last chapter, why, it may be asked, should we concern ourselves with ethics at all? If the universe is really a unity which is a spiritual organism, if this everyday world of many different things is, as a consequence, not entirely real, why should it matter how we behave in it? It is notorious that many Hindu philosophers, notably Saṁkara, have stigmatized this world as 'māyā,' that is, as illusion. The illusion is, as Hegel would say, due to the partial vision of our finite and fallible minds. But if this world is an illusion, so is our life in it. How, then,

[1] *The Religion we Need*, p. 9.

can any mistakes of conduct that we may make have more than an illusory significance?

Radhakrishnan's answer, which will be found in the first chapter on the Hindu Dharma in *The Hindu View of Life*, is that the view of this world as an illusion is not strictly Śaṃkara's view at all, although ill-advised utterances by his followers admittedly lend countenance to it. Whether it is Śaṃkara's view or not, it is assuredly not Radha-krishnan's. Given a world of subjects and objects, of knowing minds and things known, given, in fact, that the dualism between subject and object, knower and known is final, then, if reality be in its ultimate nature such as Radhakrishnan asserts, the everyday view of it as a collection of objects extended in space must be illusory. But if Radhakrishnan is right, the distinction between subject and object, knowing minds and things known is, as we have seen,[1] not ultimate, the dualism of mind and objects known to mind is not final. On the contrary, knowing mind and objects known are two sides of a unity which embraces and transcends them. This unity, Radhakrishnan teaches, is in the last resort the Absolute.

Now if mind is one side of a unity, the ideas which arise in it cannot be unrelated to that unity. Inevitably they will reflect it. And they will reflect it not merely because they arise in mind which is one of the aspects of it, but also because they come into being as the result of the interaction between mind

[1] See Chapter II, p. 65.

and the other aspect of the unity, which is not mind but object. Thus "our idea of God is the result of the interaction between subject and object. It is not the apprehension of the real object by a real subject."[1] The same is true of our idea of the world; even if it is not wholly true in the sense of containing the whole truth, this idea is not, therefore, false. It is the view of one aspect of the whole taken within the whole by another of its aspects. Therefore this aspect reflects the whole in precisely the way in which any other of its aspects reflects it. In whatever sense, then, our minds or our selves are real, in that sense the everyday world which in ordinary experience is revealed to our minds is real also. Because its reality is not ultimate the world is not, therefore, illusory. Therefore our conduct in it has a more than illusory significance.

II. Intuitional Ethics

ABSENCE OF A FORMULATED SYSTEM OF ETHICS

The possibility of ethics being vindicated, we should next proceed to an account of the particular system which Radhakrishnan advocates. But the account cannot be given, for there is no system. In two beautifully written chapters—in my view the plums of the book—in *An Idealist View of Life*, entitled "The Spirit of Man" and "Human Personality and its Destiny," Radhakrishnan discourses upon the main themes of ethics, duty and right,

[1] *The Religion we Need*, p. 24.

freedom and immortality. Yet in these two chapters, ninety-five pages in length, the section devoted to ethics proper, entitled "Intuitional and Ethical Life," occupies but two and a half. The reason is not far to seek. The basis of Radhakrishnan's thought is intuitional; it is by intuition, trained and disciplined, that, as we have seen, we achieve truth, know Beauty, attain Goodness. It is by intuition, enriched by meditation and sharpened by discipline, that we sense these three values as aspects of the Being of God. The values realized in this way become dynamic forces. God, as we have seen, is immanent in ourselves; He is the very core and essence of our being. And, since God once apprehended by the spirit begins to work in and through the spirit that apprehends Him, to realize the values as aspects of God, to realize, in fact, that God *is* the unity of the three values, is to realize the divine in ourselves.

Thus it may be said that, in so far as we apprehend God, we grow in virtue of our apprehension God-like, the potentially divine in us becoming actual: "The religious man lives in a new world which fills his mind with light, his heart with joy and his soul with life. God is seen as light, love and life."[1] This, says Radhakrishnan, is what Spinoza meant by the *amor dei intellectualis*. But, if the basis of ethics is intuitional, its object to realize goodness as "the thought of God,"[2] ethics, it is clear, can have little to do with codes and rules.

[1] *An Idealist View of Life*, p. 201.
[2] Ibid., p. 199.

The theory which Radhakrishnan proceeds on this basis to expound is, in fact, that of the moral rebel. Not merely are codes and rules indifferent to true morality; they are, he thinks, often antagonistic to it.

THE SO-CALLED MORALITY OF CONVENTION

What society calls morality is behaviour according to certain fixed moral rules. These, having been imposed upon us without the consent of our reason, are accepted on trust from the society to which we happen to belong. Most men are incapable of reflecting upon, still less of deciding moral issues for themselves, and not only incapable but unwilling. Moral freedom brings for the average man an intolerable burden; hence he shoulders the burden from his own back on to that of Society, transferring to it the task of making his morals and his beliefs for him. What most men think on moral as on political matters, about religion as about science, depends entirely upon the society into which they happen to have been born; it is an accident of topography. Getting his morals and religion, as he gets his clothes and books, ready-made from the social shop, the average man believes in Jehovah, Jesus and monogamy, if he is born in a bedroom in Balham, as surely as he believes in Allah, Mohammed and—provided he is rich enough to afford the luxury—polygamy, if he is born in a bedroom in Baghdad. As J. S. Mill points out in his *Essay on Liberty*, "it never troubles him that mere accident has decided which of these numerous (beliefs) is the object of his reliance, and that the same causes which make him a Christian in London would have made him a Buddhist or a Confucian in Pekin." His concern, in short, is not with the truth of his system of beliefs, or the rectitude of his code of morals; it is enough that there should be a system and a code. Nor in the contemporary world of the West in which, to quote Mill again, "people feel sure not so much that their opinions are true, as that they should not know what to do without them," has the position radically changed. Men's need for a code and a creed is in no way diminished merely because the scepticism of the age has destroyed the ability to satisfy the need of such moral percepts as are available.

WHY CONVENTIONAL ETHICS ARE NOT ENOUGH

Now with ethics in this sense, with ethics, that is, as a system of conventional creeds and codes, Radhakrishnan has little patience, because he denies that in any true sense it is ethics at all. Social morality, he sees clearly enough, is merely the habit of acting in conformity with certain fixed rules, those, namely, which the community has laid down for its own protection. Urged to obey by prudence, we are deterred from disobedience by fear. By conformity we win the good opinion of our neighbours; we avoid social mistakes, even if we do not soar. Such morality he stigmatizes as machine-made; his attitude to it is, indeed, almost Nietzschean in its contempt. Perfected and imposed by the mass in its own interests, it has all the characteristics and the defects of the standardized product: "Society judges all acts according to well-known common standards. It assumes that everything is susceptible of scientific or impersonal treatment. It regards men as machines and reduces every personal problem to general terms, and decides the moral worth of individual acts in the light of typical situations and moral formulas."[1]

But if we are interested in doing right, and not merely in avoiding doing wrong, this is not enough. Now to do right we must have moral freedom, freedom, that is, to develop our moral selves. And to develop our moral selves is to follow our moral intuitions.

IN WHAT SENSE MORALITY IS KNOWLEDGE

Now, for Radhakrishnan, as for Socrates, moral intuition is a form of knowledge; it is knowledge of the good which, as we have seen, is conceived as an aspect of God. In daily life, admittedly, our actions are normally automatic, being derived from respect for conventions. Every situation, every duty, every task is, nevertheless, capable of engaging *the whole self* in us. We are capable, in other words, of responding to every situation not merely with the unthinking, superficial, conventional self, which does what it does because others do the same, but with our whole being. Now it is just this whole self, the integration

[1] *An Idealist View of Life*, p. 197.

of all our powers and faculties, which is the moral self, as it is also the aesthetic self and the religious self. It is only, as we have seen, when we become fully integrated beings that we realize our spiritual natures. It is this integrated self, which is also the spiritual self, which knows its duty with "a knowledge which springs from the deeper levels of man's being."[1] To refine the spirit by discipline and meditation is to increase our ethical sensitiveness, to render, that is to say, more unerring our knowledge of the path of duty, fuller and more convincing our apprehension of the good. Responding to a situation with the whole self, integrating in the response our various energies and faculties, realizing in a word our spiritual nature, we become free. To say that we are free means that we are enabled to leave "behind the world of claims and counter claims,"[2] which constitutes the framework of what is commonly called morality.

THE ORIGINAL MORALISTS AND THE OTHERS

And not only to leave it behind, but to challenge what we leave. For the man who is gifted with direct moral insight, insisting in the light of his intuition on his freedom to pursue the good in his own way, inevitably outrages the conventional moral sense of his contemporaries. Socrates and Jesus, Buddha and Lâo-Tsze, Swedenborg, Bunyan, Blake, Ibsen, were all execrated by their contemporaries on the score

[1] *An Idealist View of Life*, p. 198.
[2] Ibid., p. 199.

of outrageous heterodoxy of belief and scandalous immorality of conduct, because they insisted on their right to follow the light which was in them—a light which we now see to have been clearer and purer than the blurred insight which condemned them—in the teeth of those preferences and prejudices which the majority pretentiously call their morals. "The moral hero follows an inner rhythm which goads him on . . . he may seem to be either unwise or unmoral to those of us who adopt the conventional standards. But for him the spiritual obligation is of more consequence than social tradition."[1] So Radhakrishnan, who proceeds after his fashion to clinch the argument with the epigram, "Though morality commands conformity, all moral progress is due to Nonconformists."[1] Realize the spirit in you, and you will apprehend the good; apprehend the good, and you will cease to rely upon conventional morals: the man of insight is a law unto himself: such, in essence, is the teaching which the preceding pages have briefly summarized.

And for those of us who are not moral seers, who have not direct insight? For us, first, there is the moral code of our community. For us, secondly, there are the examples and teaching of great men. Admittedly this teaching rarely takes the form of rules and formulae, prohibitions and prescriptions. They do not—the greatest of them—seek to confine the infinite variety of the spirit in man within the

[1] *An Idealist View of Life*, p. 197.

framework of a rigid code. This is the work, the regretted work of their followers; the priest follows the prophet, and has all too often distorted his message by formularizing it. The man of original moral insight does not announce dogmas or prescribe rules; but by attending closely to his words and studying his life, we may catch something of his spirit. Taking a hint, accepting an intimation, laying to heart a phrase or a parable, translating into the terms of one's own highest experience the higher experiences of another, one may compass the nearest thing to direct moral insight of which one's own spirit is capable. Nor need the nearest be so very, so distressingly remote; our own spirits too, partake of the divine, and all we are asked to do is to realize the divine in us. And for us, thirdly, there is the organized religion of our community to which we should turn not for the inculcation of dogma or the provision of a credo, but for the awakening of the spirit. Hereby hangs a tale, to which we shall return in the last chapter.

III. Radhakrishnan and Traditional Hindu Ethics

A QUALIFICATION

But before we turn to the next section of this one a word of qualification must be introduced. Borne along by the stream of his thought, I have come very near to presenting Radhakrishnan as a moral rebel, decrying traditions, violating codes, making light of conventions, inveighing against the accepted respectabilities. The passages from his addresses to students which concluded the first chapter cannot but have conveyed the same impression. Yet nothing *in practice* could be further from the truth. In *The Hindu View of Life* Radhakrishnan not only expounds the traditional Hindu code, a code which is, it is claimed, in practice as strict as the thought from which it springs is tolerant, broad and free, but, so far as a Western reader can judge, largely sympathizes with it. I say advisedly "so far as a Western reader can judge," because Radhakrishnan expounds so forcibly even the views with which he disagrees, that one is never quite sure of his own disagreement or by consequence of his own agreement with what he says. It is, indeed, a defect of his method, which Sir Herbert Samuel and others have pointed out, that the reader is sometimes not as clear as he would like to be whether Radhakrishnan is speaking his own mind or revealing the mind of others, or whether, when he is quite palpably doing the latter, his tacit agreement with what he is telling us is to be assumed. Yet there can, I think, be little doubt that in *The Hindu View of Life* he not only expounds but commends the traditional ethics of his countrymen.

THE HINDU *DHARMA*

The key to the Hindu system of ethics, he tells us, is the notion of *dharma*, or right action. Every form of life has its own *dharma*, which is the law of its

L

being. It is the *dharma* which holds it together, and maintains it for what it is.

Hinduism goes further and particularizes, seeking to prescribe the *dharma* or right action for the individual man. The individual's life to be rightly lived, to achieve, that is to say, a proper balance between nature and spirit, so that the life according to nature or desire may be a fitting training for the life according to the spirit, should consist of four stages. There is the student life, which is a life of preparation and training; the life of the householder, which includes marriage and citizenship; the life of retreat and the life of renunciation. Retreat begins when one's duties as a householder are finished, one's children are grown up, one's functions as a citizen performed. As the Western version has it, when one has made one's pile, it is time to retire. To retire to what? The Hindu code is unambiguous; one retires to cultivate the life of the spirit, first in retreat, which is a definite withdrawal from the society of one's fellows, then in renunciation. In renunciation man at last achieves the realization of the spirit within him; he becomes fully himself. He does not despise the world; he does not even seek to free himself from it; he becomes disinterested in it, discerning in the light of the goal which the fully realized spirit sets before itself, the comparative unimportance of the worldly ends of power, fame and wealth, for which men strive in sweating competition. Let us endeavour to translate into modern terms.

'RETIREMENT' IN THE WEST

The failure of modern life is a failure in the life of the spirit, or, as we are accustomed to put it in the West, a failure in the use of leisure. Those of us whom the world deems fortunate retire, and, as I pointed out in the Prologue, we are so little able to tolerate the resultant freedom to do what we like with our minds, souls and bodies, that after a course of big game shooting, mountain climbing, desert exploring or some other difficult and unpleasant pursuit in which they can only induce other people to accompany them by the offer of large sums of money, our rich men are driven as often as not to return to their desks and to make money which they do not want, in despair of finding life tolerable without the hard labour to which they have been accustomed. Or they take to perpetual movement, and, continually in transit over the surface of the earth or the water, seek perpetually to escape from something which is lying in wait for them in whatever place they happen to be. This something is boredom; or, if you like, the fear of having to look their own souls in the face. Thus for the rich unoccupied Westerner all places are preferable to that in which he happens to be. Or, they go and kill something, identifying the good life with depriving other creatures of life.

What emphatically they do not do is to go into retreat and prepare for the life of the spirit. This horror of physical inactivity, this inability to repose, this preoccupation with the movement of pieces of matter, in a word, this spiritual impotence of our unoccupied rich, is an extreme illustration of that radical defect of Western civilization, the ignorance of how to live the good life of which we possess so abundantly the means, upon which stress was laid in the Prologue. This defect appears as clearly in the clerk who can find no better occupation for his fortnight's holiday than to lounge on the sands at the seaside and quarrel with his wife because she does not possess the physical attractions of the stars over whom he smacks his lips during his frequent visits to the cinema, as it does in the millionaire who employs him; but as the clerk is permitted by his millionaire employer very little time in which to demonstrate his inefficiency in the art of life, and very little money with which to indulge his tastes, it is less sensationally apparent.

Thus, when in the course of the series of lectures delivered at Manchester College, Oxford, and subsequently published as *The Hindu View of Life*, Radhakrishnan lays stress upon retreat and renunciation and praises the life of the spirit, he is by his praise definitely and, as I conceive it, deliberately setting before us this aspect of the Hindu conception of the good life as at once a rebuke and an example to ourselves. The Hindus, the best of them at any rate, do know what to do with themselves when their active working life is over. By meditation, training and discipline they cultivate the spirit; we do not. Their aim is to develop their faculties, and by becoming integrated personalities, to realize all that they have it in them to be; we live and become lopsided men and women in whom the mind has been exercised and the body overnourished, to the exclusion, often to the atrophy, of the spirit.

DEFENCE OF CASTE

Even the caste system is not to be dismissed with the common casual disparagement; on the contrary, it is praised, praised not for what it has in fact become, but for what in origin and intention it once was. Caste, we are told, is really custom. The insistence upon caste is really an insistence upon the importance of preserving the separate tribal customs of the primitive peoples whom Hindu civilization has from time to time absorbed.

Hindu civilization has neither exterminated nor suppressed the various non-Hindu groups who have originated in or invaded the peninsula. It has adopted the method of democracy, incorporating them while at the same time permitting them to retain their separate individualities within the body of the whole. The primitive customs and traditions, the individual ways of life and social modes of behaviour appropriate to these peoples were retained. Modified by the superior culture in which they were incorporated, they modified it in their turn, contributing to it a new freshness and vigour.

Caste was in intention the system whereby these separate group entities were preserved and their individualities safeguarded. It was a system based on tolerance and trust. To-day, admittedly, the caste system has become a degradation, an instrument of reaction, an ally of ignorance and an excuse for oppression. Radhakrishnan is prominent among its denouncers. But it does not follow that the idea behind it is valueless, or that the system itself was to be condemned in its prime because it merits condemnation in its decline.

CHARACTERISTICS OF HINDU THOUGHT

Nor is it to be supposed, because he is so zealous an exponent of the Hindu way of life as it has been ideally lived, that Radhakrishnan approves the present state of India. At the end of *The Hindu View of Life* he is definitely critical of the sterile dogmatism in which Hindu thought has apparently come to rest. The vital flow of religious inspiration has trickled away into the sands of scholarship and formalism, and there apparently it has lost itself.

It is, indeed, difficult to read Indian philosophy with its endless commentaries upon the semi-sacred texts of its various systems without deriving the impression that one is being presented with a testimony, one of the most striking, to the perverted ingenuity of the human mind.

The situation on the face of it is puzzling. Here is a people which has been continuously engaged for centuries in the business of sustained philosophizing. Philosophy has been pursued, as naturally, as inevitably by the best brains of India as science in the contemporary West; and pursued for centuries. The result is a formidable corpus of philosophic writing containing as scattered plums in the dough of abstract theological speculation most of, or, as some claim, all the ideas which have at different times been enthusiastically acclaimed as novelties in the West, from emergence and 'holism' to the latest developments of neo-Idealism. Yet the ideas are unacknowledged in the West, the philosophy almost entirely unread. The reason is, I think—and it is relevant to give it, since it is one of Radhakrishnan's chief tasks to overcome it—the unfamiliar, the perverse form which Indian philosophers have chosen to adopt.

Indian thought is for the most part contained in systems. The form of most of the Indian systems is broadly the same. There is a set of poems or prose passages, the Vedas or the Upaniṣads, from which the system derives and upon which it is based. There are treatises written in short pregnant sentences, the *sūtras*, usually in commentary or exposition of the original poems or of the ideas contained in them. The *sūtras* being held in the greatest respect, any new thought or speculation which occurs to subsequent thinkers is announced in the form of a commentary upon or a development of the thought of the *sūtras*. It has, therefore, first to be reconciled with them, in the sense of being shown to be merely a development of ideas already latent in them, and secondly, to defend itself against the criticism advanced on behalf of rival systems. In this way the original treatises, the *sūtras*, and the commentaries upon and developments of the *sūtras*, come to form an elaborate system. As the system grows, it has to meet unexpected criticisms and to withstand the impact of new ideas for which it is not in the least prepared. Thus, to quote Dr. Dasgupta,[1] each system "grew and developed by the untiring energy of its adherents through all successive ages of history; and a history of this growth is a history of its conflicts."

WHY UNCONGENIAL TO THE WEST

The process I have recorded is quite unlike anything in Western thought, and gives to Indian philosophy an air of unfamiliarity. The original poems and prose texts consist of philosophical truths intuitively perceived, revelations of reality, which are considered to need neither argument nor defence. The *sūtras* are more like lecture notes than books. Short and pithy, they bristle with technical terms and are full of allusions to the objections brought by rival systems which they are seeking to refute. Not only are the technical terms not explained but they are used in different senses in different places, while the allusions, intelligible enough no doubt to those who had direct oral instruction on the subject, are lost upon Western readers.

Puzzled by the form of Indian philosophy, the Westerner is unable to see why it should have been adopted. Is it not, he cannot help wondering,

[1] See *A History of Indian Philosophy*, by Surendranath Dasgupta.

prejudicial to new thought to compel it to accommodate itself within the bounds of a traditional system?
Does not the veneration with which the systems are
regarded as complete compendia of truth tend to
stifle free enquiry, and to substitute scholarship and
textual criticism, dialectical skill and the ingenuity
which is required of those who must fit new pieces
into old frameworks, for the free play of the un-
fettered mind? The Westerner finds the implied criticism of these reflections confirmed by Dr. Dasgupta.

"All the independence of their thinking was
limited and enchained by the faith of the school to
which they were attached. Instead of producing a
succession of free-lance thinkers having their own
system to propound and establish, India had brought
forth schools of pupils who carried the traditional
views of particular systems from generation to
generation, who explained and expounded them,
and defended them against the attacks of other
rival schools which they constantly attacked in
order to establish the superiority of the system to
which they adhered."

The history of the systems extends for about two
thousand years. Their development seems to have
stopped about the beginning of the seventeenth
century, and with the development of the systems
Indian philosophy itself seems to have come to a
standstill.

Contemplating this curious corpus of dogma, piety
and learning the Western reader is doubly repelled.
So far as the past is concerned, he finds the ideas,

the undoubtedly valuable ideas, of Indian philosophy clothed in the unfamiliar and forbidding garb of a commentary upon sacred texts; so far as concerns the present, he is led to suppose that philosophy has reached a dead end. The waters of speculation have, he is given to understand, ceased to flow; there has been, in fact, no living thought for a couple of hundred years. And yet, if Radhakrishnan is to be believed, the period of stagnation is drawing to a close. The appearance of apathy is only in part trustworthy. It is true that listlessness is still all too often the characteristic of Hindu thought as well as life, but forces making for change are at work, change which constitutes not a break with but a development of the Hindu tradition. Such change there has in fact always been, a continuing leaven of vitality fermenting within the matrix of Hindu thought. "There has been no such thing as a uniform, stationary, unalterable Hinduism, whether in point of belief or practice. Hinduism is a movement not a position; a process not a result; a growing tradition not a fixed revelation."[1]

The present marks the end of one epoch, the beginning of another. In India, as elsewhere, men live in a stage of transition, looking to the coming of a new world before they are finally quit of the old one.

RADHAKRISHNAN'S OWN POSITION

Of the "New Hinduism," as it has been called, Radhakrishnan is a prominent exponent. In this

[1] *The Hindu View of Life*, p. 129.

sense, perhaps, he might be called a rebel against the old. But the word 'rebel' is a misnomer, for in his case there has been no break with the old. Rather he has sought to pour the wine of new thought into the skins of an old tradition. He is an innovator, and, what is more, a developing innovator; but always the development he sponsors takes place within the matrix of the Hindu attitude to life from which, he would say, it derives its inspiration. Radhakrishnan is not in any real sense of the word a rebel; he accepts the traditions of his people, its traditions of thought as of life, believing that they "will be found equal to any emergency that the future may throw up, whether on the field of thought or of history,"[1] seeking only to develop them in the light of new needs, and to apply them to new situations.

I have inserted this section because I wanted to correct the possible impression left by the conclusion of the first chapter and by the preceding sections of this one that Radhakrishnan is a heterodox Hindu, throwing overboard the secular ethics of his race, and appealing to a personal intuition to justify revolt against a collective and traditional wisdom. This is emphatically not the case. On the contrary Radhakrishnan, as I pointed out in my first chapter, adopts of set purpose the rôle of spokesman for the East, offering its traditional wisdom as a specific to compose the distraction and aimlessness of the West. Admittedly, he is not content to leave that

[1] *The Hindu View of Life*, p. 130.

wisdom as he found it; admittedly he seeks to vitalize, to develop and to apply in new ways the traditional Hindu attitude. But in all essentials it remains his attitude, and because it is *secular* rather than contemporary, because it is an inheritance rather than an acquirement, a collective wisdom rather than a personal contribution, I shall say no more about it here, but pass to matters upon which Radhakrishnan's thought is in a more distinctive and individual sense his own.

IV. Karma and the Freedom of Man

I come now to the more characteristic and personal part of Radhakrishnan's ethical teaching. The view of ethics as intuitional outlined in the second section, presupposes—it is obvious—that man is free. Freedom is, indeed, the very essence of the indwelling spirit in man, which is also, as we have seen, the spirit of an immanent God. Can this postulate of Man's freedom be granted, and how can it be made to square with the doctrine of Karma which Radhakrishnan as a good Hindu is prepared to sponsor?

The doctrine of Karma as expounded by Radhakrishnan has two aspects; a deterministic and a free willist, each of which is the complement of the other. For the purpose of exposition these two aspects must be considered separately. It must, however, be borne in mind that this separation is for convenience of exposition only; each considered by itself is an abstraction from the truth; the truth is in the two together.

A. THE DETERMINIST SIDE OF KARMA

The determinist element may be stated very simply. The course of nature is determined by immutable laws. "The universe," Radhakrishnan agrees with the scientists—although not with the most modern doctrines of some physicists—"is lawful to the core."[1] This lawfulness applies also to human nature; its development too is subject to law and conditioned by immutable principles. But the kind of necessity to which human nature is subject is different from the mechanism of physical law which operates in the world of inanimate matter. It is a spiritual rather than a mechanical necessity: "Karma is not a mechanical principle but a spiritual necessity. It is the embodiment of the word and will of God. God is its supervisor."[2] And the necessity is just this, that, as a man has sown, so shall he reap.

The principle of Karma is a principle of justice. A man's thought and action in one life is conditioned by the potency exerted by his thoughts and actions in previous lives; conditioned at least, until he can liquidate the potency by knowledge, contemplation, and strict adherence to the five great vows. For it

[1] *The Hindu View of Life*, p. 72.
[2] Ibid., p. 73.

is always open to a man to liquidate his past Karma, and, provided that no more Karma is generated, to break the chain of birth and rebirth which the potency of past Karma entails.

Theoretically, then, and at the end freedom may be achieved; freedom is, indeed, not only at the end; it is the end.

But meanwhile and in practice the doctrine looks to Western eyes suspiciously like a purely passive Fatalism. Nothing, we are assured, can efface our past Karma; it determines the conditions and the framework of our lives; it provides the raw material of our characters. A man's character, in fact, is conditioned by all the actions which he has performed in the past, the past not only of one life but of many. Admittedly, I am assured that by the exercise of will and resolution leading to right thought and right action extending over a number of lives, I may break the chain of causes and consequences and liquidate the Karma of my past lives. But this assurance brings little comfort. For whence, I cannot help asking, are to be derived the will and the resolution necessary to acquire the power of right thought and the habit of right action? If a man is free, free *before* he has liquidated his Karma, well and good; no difficulty arises and he can at any moment begin the new life which the Indian sage enjoins. But how, then, one is tempted to ask, represent him as at the same time determined by the fruits of past Karma which he is reaping?

SELF-DETERMINISM

Viewed in the light of these and similar considerations, the doctrine of Karma comes to the Westerner to bear a striking resemblance to determinism; to that form of determinism which he has learnt from Aristotle to call self-determinism.

Let us paraphrase Aristotle's statement of it.

A man, says Aristotle, comes to have a good character because he has continually performed good acts. But he cannot continually perform good acts unless he is the sort of man whose nature it is to perform them, unless, that is to say, he possesses the good character from which the good acts necessarily spring. This good character will, in its turn, proceed from and be formed by a preceding series of good acts. Retracing our steps by this method over the past history of the individual, we conclude that the actions which he performs at any given moment spring from, and are conditioned by, his being the sort of person that he is at that moment, and, further, that he is the particular sort of person that he then is, because of the impulses which he experiences, the desires which he entertains and the tendencies which he exhibits. If, therefore, we carry our analysis far enough back, we can show that the tendencies, desires and impulses which were originally his on the first occasion on which he acted are those which really determined the whole subsequent tenor of his life. If we leave out of account, as Aristotle does, the bearing upon the issue of theories of rebirth we must admit that the tendencies, desires and impulses which the individual possesses on the first occasion on which he acts lie outside his control. These tendencies, desires and impulses, which we are accustomed to call hereditary, operating in relation to and reacting upon the environment in which he finds himself, determine his future actions. By these actions his character is formed. But, since on this view he is responsible neither for his hereditary equipment nor for his environment, it would appear that he is not accountable either for the actions which these two factors jointly determine or for the character which is formed by these actions.

INSTINCTIVE DETERMINISM OF THE WESTERN MIND

Now this doctrine of self-determinism has become to all intents and purposes the accepted view of the West. Reinforced by psycho-analysis, which has given it a pseudo-scientific backing, it has passed into the common intellectual stock-in-trade of the ordinary Western man. He really believes that he is not free, although paradoxically he holds that the series of judgments as a result of which this belief of his has been built up have been formed as the result of a disinterested and dispassionate analysis, by a mind 'freely' considering the available evidence. Just as I find it taken for granted by students who are starting philosophy for the first time that only material things are real, so do I find an instinctive assumption that free will is a myth.

This instinctive determinism takes one or other of three forms, each of which is appropriate to a particular science. A man, it is held, is determined either jointly by his heredity and his environment (biology), or by his brain, body and nervous system (physiology), or by the unconscious desires and urges whose sublimated versions form the contents of consciousness (psychology). But, while all the sciences have played their part, it is recent developments in psychology which are chiefly responsible for the formation of this instinctive attitude.

DETERMINIST INFLUENCE OF MODERN PSYCHOLOGY

Much modern psychology is thoroughly determinist in outlook; it tends to throw doubt upon the uniqueness of man's mind and to deny the freedom of his will. This result comes about in two different ways. In the first place, Behaviourism has achieved unexpected success in interpreting the behaviour of human beings without introducing the assumption that they have minds. They may have, of course, for, since a mind cannot be observed, to deny it is, it is held, as unreasonable as to assert it; but, if they have, there is no reason to think that their minds influence their behaviour.

This, at least, is the assertion of the Behaviourists. Beginning with a study of animal psychology, they reached certain conclusions tending to show that animals were automata. These conclusions nobody felt impelled to resist, since few supposed that animals were virtuous and fewer still had any interest in maintaining that they possessed minds. The Behaviourists then proceeded to apply their conclusions to human beings, who were humiliated to find how mindless they could be made to appear, but were, nevertheless, unable to produce very convincing reasons for supposing that they were not the highly complicated automata which the Behaviourists represented them to be. Pavlov's celebrated study of the conditioned reflexes of dogs made our automatism more credible by showing how and why simple physical stimuli could produce such catastrophic and apparently irrelevant responses, as when the receipt of a sheet of paper bearing the imprint of a black hand causes the victim in a boy's crook story to go and throw himself over the edge of a cliff. A difficult proposition, one would have supposed, to explain the suicide response to the black hand stimulus without supposing that the victim had a mind which grasped the *import*, the *significance*, of the black hand; but Pavlov's work enables us to see how it can be done without assuming that the victim is anything but body. It is, indeed, precisely this proposition that human beings are *all* body and *only* body that the Behaviourists have very ably advocated and, if it could be successfully maintained, it would, it is clear, imply a denial of the freedom of our wills and the spontaneity of our spirits. The laws which govern the behaviour of our bodies are known. Primarily they are those of mechanics and dynamics, secondly those of chemistry, ultimately those of physics. Given a knowledge of these laws, the movements of the body like those of any other piece of matter can be predicted. If, then, we are all body. . . . The conclusion is all too clear.

IMPLICATIONS OF PSYCHO-ANALYSIS

In the second place, the theories of psycho-analysts, while not casting doubt upon the existence of mind, clearly demonstrate the dependence of its rational upon its non-rational elements. Consciousness, they maintain, is for the most part nothing but a screen put up by the unconscious to save our *amour propre*; conscious events are the distorted reflections of unconscious desires and impulses, and what we think, feel and do is determined not *by* us but *for* us by forces deep down in the recesses of our personalities, whose genesis escapes detection and whose workings evade control.

Modern psychology proper, while rejecting the somewhat bizarre machinery of psycho-analysis, issues in the works of many writers in not dissimilar conclusions. It is, that is to say, fundamentally irrationalist in tendency, sees in instinct and impulse the mainspring of our personalities and exhibits reason and will as mere corks bobbing on the waves of desire.

On this view reason is the handmaid of our instincts, not the arbiter of our destinies; its function is to provide us with justifications for what we instinctively wish to believe and pretexts for what we instinctively want to do, while the will is no less enslaved to elements in our natures which we do not control and for which we cannot be held responsible.

If we are not ultimately responsible for what we think or what we do, if our natures are formed not *by* us but *for* us, free will, it is clear, is a delusion. We are automata no less on the psycho-analyst view than on the behaviourist; we are determined, it is true, not by our bodily responses to external stimuli, but by instinctive trends of which we are unconscious; but we are determined none the less for that.

Thus the implications of contemporary psychology, in so far as it is represented by the two important schools of thought at which I have glanced, are definitely determinist. Mind, it seems, is not unique; freedom is an illusion; ethics is a rationalization of non-ethical impulses; purpose and design are figments; living organisms are no less automata than machines. Also, modern psychology is very popular and has profoundly affected people's unconscious modes of thinking.

I emphasize this instinctive determinism of Western thought and the factors chiefly responsible for engendering it, because it affords a good example of the particular mood to which, while he regards it as mistaken, Radhakrishnan's message from the East is specially addressed. Not only does he devote many of the critical pages of *An Idealist View of Life* to an examination of this mood and of the attitude in which it finds expression, but it is in contradistinction to it that he urges most strongly his own doctrine of freedom.

HOW OUTSTRIPPED BY EASTERN THOUGHT

'That there is a deterministic side to human nature,' he says, in effect, 'the East could always have told you. The doctrine of Karma,—as you will have observed from my sketch—makes full allowance for this deterministic strain in human thought and action upon which, incited thereto by science, you lay such stress. Why, then, this flutter in the dovecotes, as at the announcement of a new and shattering truth, merely because science has dotted the i's and crossed the t's of conclusions which have been a commonplace of Eastern thought for generations? Why, in fact, all this fuss? We have not only made terms with determinism, we have extended its aegis further than you have ever dreamed of doing, asserting the determining influence of the past not of one life but of many, perhaps of an infinite series of past lives. The view that your infantile erotic desire for your nurse should have determined your present aversion from pickled cabbage, and your incestuous feeling for your mother, your present inability to spell, seems to be the limit of your psycho-analysts' imaginations. But how if it was your profligacy as a courtier in the Middle Ages, or as a courtesan in ancient Babylon, or even maybe your behaviour in connection with those cave drawings in Cromagnon days, that is responsible for your present aberrations? For this and nothing less is what the doctrine of Karma implies. And yet we have always known in the East that these determining factors from the past are not the whole story; not by a long way!'

But before I complete the story by the introduction of the complementary element of freedom, it will be as well to summarize in outline Radhakrishnan's individual teaching on the vexed question of rebirth. Does the individual, it may be asked, really live many lives? If so, how can he, since he occupies a different body in each of them and since the body, on any view, largely determines the complexion of the spirit, be the same individual in each of them?

THE DOCTRINE OF REBIRTH

Radhakrishnan's position in regard to this difficult question may be summarized under six heads. The first four consist of his reasons for believing in rebirth.

(1) Nature bears witness to a process of incessant renewal. At the zoological level this process appears to be concerned solely for the perpetuation of species. At the human level of development the perpetuation of individuality seems to be the end in view. Therefore, the reasons for believing in the renewal of species through many individuals at the biological level are also reasons for believing in the renewal of an individual through many lives at the human level.

(2) Nature bears witness to continuity; to con-

tinuity, that is, within a general pattern. Everything arises from and passes into something which is continuous with it. There is no apparent reason why human selves should be regarded as exceptions to this principle. If they are not, they must continue: "They carry on past threads, weave out something in the present, and prepare for the future."[1]

(3) The object of the self is the "fulfilment of function or development of individuality."[1] This object cannot be secured in one life. We do not—the fact is, alas, only too obvious—develop all our powers or achieve all our ends. But, once grant that our chance of self-fulfilment continues indefinitely into the future, and this need cause no disquietude: "There are no blind rushes to the goal";[1] there is a connected sequence in which "the acts of one life determine the basis and opportunities of the next."[1]

(4) "It is an admitted principle of science that, if we see a certain stage of development in time, we may infer a past to it."[2] We appear in the world not as clean slates for the writing of environment and circumstance, but as slates already inscribed. For example, we inherit talents, "an eye for beauty, a taste for music, which are not common qualities of the species but individual variations."[2] "We cannot believe that the rise of self with a definite nature is simply fortuitous";[2] therefore, we must presuppose a past for the self, in which the individual inheritance

---

[1] *An Idealist View of Life*, p. 288.
[2] Ibid., p. 289.

which it brings with it into the world has been built up. This is McTaggart's famous argument for pre-existence. Infant prodigies in music or chess constitute its most striking illustrations. Assuming the fact to be established, Radhakrishnan next proceeds to consider the nature of the machinery which must be postulated to account for the fact.

(5) THE PROBLEM OF MIND-BODY ASSOCIATION

How does a particular soul come to be incarnated in a particular body? To this question no exact or even plausible answer can be given. But, as Radhakrishnan points out, unless and until we can give a satisfactory account of the relation between a body and a mind, the difficulty is not peculiar to the theory of rebirth. A human being is, we are provisionally assuming, not all body; if he is all body, then materialism gives a correct account of him and this whole discussion falls to the ground. Yet obviously he is, or rather has, a body; his body, then, is animated by a mind. Granted, again, that we reject the materialist view that the character of the mind or self is *entirely determined*, although admittedly it is *influenced* by the body, then some other origin must be sought for the peculiarities of the individual self. To reveal this origin is a problem for any psychology; it is not, I repeat the point, a peculiar difficulty for the theory of rebirth. For in some way—the fact must be admitted, even though it cannot be explained—minds are associated with bodies; in some sense, then, minds, seeing that they exhibit characteristics which are not entirely due to their associations with bodies, must pre-exist them. How, then, do they become associated?

The traditional Hindu answer is that in addition to the ordinary physical body there is another, the *liṅgaśarīra* or subtle body which, accompanying the ordinary body through its physical existence, nevertheless survives it. The *liṅgaśarīra* is the framework or mould upon which the body is formed, and, when the time for rebirth comes, attracts to itself those physical elements which can be accommodated within the framework to form the new physical body. Thus, if rebirth is the renewal of the instrument of the physical body through which the self works, the *liṅgaśarīra* is the continuing tool by means of which the new instrument is fashioned. Fashioned by the self(?) Or by whom or what? We are not told.

Radhakrishnan, indeed, does not press this suggestion, which in the nature of things must remain sheer hypothesis, but it is, as I understand it, a traditional Hindu doctrine which he is prepared to regard as constituting at least as plausible an account of the matter as any other which has been suggested.

(6) REBIRTH AND HEREDITY

Something must be said of the bearing upon the theory of rebirth of the question of heredity. Here an obvious difficulty suggests itself. The child resembles the parents often in mind as well as in body. Is it not reasonable to suppose, then, that it proceeds entirely from them, and that, just as its body is the stuff of their bodies, so its mind is an emanation from their minds? But, if it is, what becomes of the theory of rebirth?

Radhakrishnan points out that this difficulty applies to any theory except a purely materialistic one. If we hold that each soul is a brand-new creation by God, there is still the difficulty of understanding why it should bear so palpably upon it the traces of the parents. Moreover, to hold that a soul of super-natural essence is thrust by divine agency into a bodily form at a specific moment of time savours of the fantastic and even, as Lucretius insisted, of the absurd. His comic picture of souls standing in queues waiting for vacant bodies to enter is unforgettable. Speaking for my part, it sufficed to kill this view with ridicule once and for all.

Radhakrishnan, following up the hint of the *lingaśarīra*, makes the following suggestion. A self which is seeking for rebirth becomes embodied in the bodily structure which is most suitable for that particular self. What does 'most suitable' mean? A bodily structure which fits most appropriately into the mould of the subtle body, the *lingaśarīra*, which persists from life to life. "The self selects the frame which fits it, even as we pick the hat which suits the shape of our head. We are reborn in families where the qualities we possess and seek to embody are well developed."[1]

Thus our physical bodies in different lives tend

[1] *An Idealist View of Life*, p. 296.

to resemble each other for the reason that each has to accommodate itself to the framework of the continuing "subtle body," or, perhaps, because the self deliberately chooses those bodily forms which most closely approximate to the continuing mould. Whatever suggestion is made must in the nature of things be the merest hypothesis. But a theory which suggests that there is a necessary reason for a certain degree of resemblance between successive physical bodies inhabited by the same self, has the advantage of enabling us to answer the question posed above,[1] "How, if the body determines at least in part the nature of the self, can it really be the same self which is incarnated in different bodies?" The answer is that the bodies are not themselves radically different but tend to resemble each other; and they resemble each other because they have, as it were, to pass through the sieve of the *liṅgaśarīra*, with the result that only those which are suited to the self get through.

We are now in a position to turn to the free-will element in the doctrine of Karma, the element in virtue of which the determinism upon which we have hitherto dwelt can never be either final or supreme.

B. THE FREE WILLIST SIDE OF KARMA

The free-will element in the doctrine of Karma may be stated as follows. Nothing, it is agreed, can efface our past Karma; it persists as an element in our present, and, so persisting, conditions our

[1] See p. 182.

future. It conditions, but it does not determine.
For man is an embodiment of a spiritual principle
which is by its very nature a principle of freedom.
And to say that his spirit is or includes freedom is
to say also that he can at any moment transcend the
limits imposed by his Karma, and break the chain
which his past lives and actions have forged.

"While it regards the past as determined, it" (the
doctrine of Karma) "allows that the future is only
conditioned. The spiritual element in a man allows
him freedom within the limits of his nature. Man is
not a mere mechanism of instincts. The spirit in
him can triumph over the automatic forces that try
to enslave him."[1]

Before I come to a more detailed statement of Radhakrishnan's doctrine, I will give in my own words
what I conceive to be the essence of his teaching
on this difficult question. Or rather, I will summarize
a statement, celebrated in the history of philosophy,
which strikes precisely the same balance between
the claims of determinism and freedom as that for
which Radhakrishnan seems to me to be contending.

PLATO'S STATEMENT OF FREE WILL

I have already remarked how often in reading
Radhakrishnan one is struck by reminiscences of
Platonic doctrine. His theory of free will affords the
most striking of these reminiscences. Plato's *Republic*
closes with a celebrated myth, the myth of Er. The
myth of Er is a vision of the soul's fate after death.

[1] *The Hindu View of Life*, p. 75.

Er is taken to a spot to which the souls proceed immediately after death to be judged. There are two streams of souls, the first travelling to heaven or hell for a thousand years of bliss or punishment according to their deserts, the second returning after their sojourn in heaven or hell to choose a new life on earth. The choice which the souls make is the all-important crisis in their history. Into it there enter two factors, one of necessity, the second, that of freedom. In the first place, the order in which the souls choose is determined for them by lot; herein is the element of chance. But, secondly, however late in the order a soul gets its choice, it still has a choice, so that even the soul that chooses last, when all the best available lives might be considered to have been already snapped up, may still, provided it chooses wisely, obtain a life worth living. Once the soul has made its choice of life, it has chosen its destiny; thus a man's own will becomes his destiny in the sense that he can never reverse what he has once chosen or the consequences of his choice. Moreover, in making his choice his will is influenced, although never determined, by his past life and past choices. For example, souls who have spent a thousand years in Purgatory generally return wiser for what they have undergone, so that they choose a humble life of wisdom and good works rather than a life of glory and power. Conversely, the enjoyment of a thousand years of bliss sometimes leads a soul to make a worse choice than it otherwise would have done. In another dialogue, the *Phaedrus*, we are told that, if a soul after the enjoyment of bliss makes a wise choice and continues to do so on successive occasions, living better in each life and becoming better through repeated sojourns in heaven, it escapes at last the necessity of putting on a material body and, freed from the necessity of further choosing of lives, remains a pure soul.

Four points may be emphasized in this doctrine. The first three are determinist. First, circumstances (in the myth the circumstance of the lot) influence choices; secondly, a choice once made determines one's destiny and is irrevocable. Thirdly, a choice is not only limited by circumstances but influenced by the past history of the chooser. The purport of the myth of Er is to insist that what is done by the soul upon earth has a direct effect upon its future. Thus the doctrine of the immortality of the soul, involving, as it does, the continuity of its existence, adds to our moral responsibility and increases the importance of living rightly. The concluding words of the *Republic* emphasize the fact that the one thing needful is to study how to make oneself better and wiser not only for this life but in order that, when one's turn comes to choose another, one may make a correct choice for one's future. Life on earth, in fact, is, rightly regarded, a process of learning and training for that future. The fourth point emphasizes the fact of freedom. In spite of all, the soul *really is free*; the past influences and inclines, ~~but~~ *but* never necessitates its choice.

THE HINDU VIEW OF FREEDOM

Plato, so far as I know, was not directly influenced by the teaching of the East. Nevertheless, it is difficult to avoid being struck by the resemblance between this account of freedom and that of Hindu philosophy. The main points of resemblance seem to be these. First, a man's choice once made is irrevocable; it determines his destiny in respect of that which he has chosen, and must needs, therefore, influence all future choices. As the Eastern view puts it, a man having chosen is bound to feel the effects of his choice from the causes he has himself set in motion. Every time a man chooses evil his character is determined by the fact of his choice, and this determination makes it easier for him to choose evil and harder to choose good on the next occasion on which a choice presents itself. In this sense, then, it is true that our choices, in determining our actions, determine also our characters, and to this extent influence our future choices.

But, and this is the second point, they never necessitate them. Although it becomes harder for me to choose good each time I choose evil, it never becomes impossible. For choice is always free, and no amount of choosing in the past, although it may bias and influence can ever necessitate a present choice.

Now let us put the point in Radhakrishnan's own words. "Our demand for freedom must reckon with a universe that is marked by order and regularity. Life is like a game of bridge. The cards in the game are given to us. We do not select them. They are traced to past Karma, but we are free to make any call as we think fit and lead any suit. Only we are limited by the rules of the game. We are more free when we start the game than later on when the game has developed and our choices become restricted. But till the very end there is always a choice. A good player will see possibilities which a bad one does not. The more skilled a player the more alternatives does he perceive. A good hand may be cut to pieces by unskilful play and the bad play need not be attributed to the frowns of fortune."[1]

The cards with which we have to play, our temperament, disposition, character, "are given to us. We do not select them. They are traced to past Karma." Exactly; the activity of our freedom, it is obvious, is confined within the framework imposed upon us by our past. Moreover, "we are limited by the rules of the game"; that is, we are born into an environment which restricts the number of choices we can make. Because of this environment only certain possibilities are open. Here, then, are the two great determining factors; the one, our past Karma determining the nature of the raw material at our disposal, the character with which and in which we have to work; the second, the environment which determines our opportunities of utilizing our character. Yet within these limits "we

[1] *An Idealist View of Life,* p. 279.

are free to make any call as we think fit and lead any suit."

THE ENVIRONMENT NOT SEPARATE FROM
THE INDIVIDUAL

There is a further aspect of this doctrine of freedom which must be mentioned. I have represented the individual as being determined by his environment, as if the environment were a thing separate and apart, into which the individual was pitchforked much as one pitchforks hay into a yard. But such a conception ignores the theory of knowledge at which in Chapter II we have already glanced. Subject and object, we there saw, constitute a unity. Both are aspects of this unity; in it alone they have being; divorced from it they are abstractions. The same may be said of the self and its environment.

"The real whole or individual is that which includes persons and their environment and these exist in themselves by a process," and, we may add, *only* by a process, "of abstraction. . . . The individual and the world coexist and subsist together."[1]

The view of the individual as forming an integral part of his environment, as being, in fact, not wholly real apart from it, has been advocated by Professor J. S. Haldane from the side of biology. Radhakrishnan is familiar with Haldane's views and quotes from Haldane's book *The Sciences and Philosophy* in illustration of his own doctrine. "Personality

[1] *An Idealist View of Life*, p. 272.

is not something confined and complete in itself separately from an environment in space and time, but extends over that environment."[1] This conception is not altogether an easy one, and a brief exposition may serve a useful purpose in showing its relevance to the issues under discussion.

PROFESSOR J. S. HALDANE'S VIEWS

Haldane was led to his view by his inability to accept either of the two modes of explanation currently put forward in the philosophy of biology, the mechanist and the vitalist. The arguments against Mechanism are well known and need not be repeated here. The difficulty of Vitalism is that, since the vital force which it invokes can neither be located in nor separated from the living organism, it runs the risk of being dismissed as sheer hypothesis, a limited *deus ex machina* invented by biologists in a difficulty and discredited by the impossibility of conceiving interaction between the material and the immaterial, and by the fact that modern research shows ever more plainly that events within the organism are ultimately dependent upon and conditioned by circumstances outside it. The inference is that any particular case in which the dependence cannot be made out is due to inadequate knowledge rather than to the arbitrary interference of a vital principle.

For these reasons the question with which biologists, both mechanist and vitalist, have so frequently

[1] J. S. Haldane, *The Sciences and Philosophy*, p. 303.

concerned themselves, "Does the organism influence the environment or the environment the organism?" is really unanswerable; and it is unanswerable just becauses it presupposes a radical separation between organism and environment. In fact, however, the organism cannot be separated from its environment, since, in Professor Haldane's view, "The conception of life embraces the environment of an organism, as well as what is within its body."[1] "Organism and external environment hang together," says Professor Haldane, "in the specific manner which is a normal expression of the life of the organism. . . . There is no spatial limit to the life of the organism, just as there is no spatial limit to what can be perceived."[2] The notion of an organism extending all over its environment is inconceivable so long as our imaginations are limited by the nineteenth-century conception of things as consisting of separate bits of matter extended in space. Physics, however, has abandoned this view, and, as Professor Haldane points out, is adopting a conception of the atom not dissimilar from that which he is putting forward for the living organism. The modern atom is the sum-total of the influences which it exerts over its environment, just as a living organism is conceived as being, or at any rate as extending over, the environment whose co-operation is necessary to the maintenance of its activity. Thus biological conceptions are increasingly invading physics. We

[1] J. S. Haldane, *The Philosophical Basis of Biology*, p. 18.
[2] Ibid., p. 74.

no longer think of a living body as made up of atoms of inert matter which by some miracle come alive, but rather of the ultimate constituents of matter as entities which, in refusing to be divorced or conceived apart from their environment, demand to be interpreted in terms of concepts appropriate to life.

And so we reach the general conclusion which Professor Haldane shares with Professor Whitehead, that "behind the appearance of a physical world there exists a world in the interpretation of which biological principles must be applied."[1]

I have summarized the views of Professor Haldane in some little detail because the use which Radhakrishnan makes of them in expounding his doctrine of freedom affords a good illustration of his talent for pouring the new wine of Western thought into the old bottles of Eastern wisdom. The East has always known that man was free; the doctrine of Karma expressed its conviction. But the West wants evidence, and, if Professor Haldane is right, may find it in the inability of its own biological science to understand how organism and environment conceived as separate and distinct entities can interact. Very well, then, the conclusion is inescapable, they are not separate and distinct entities!

Radhakrishnan sees the significance of the point, and presses it home in the interests of the free-will element in the doctrine of Karma.

[1] J. S. Haldane, *The Philosophical Basis of Biology*, p. 38.

His general teaching may now be stated as follows. To consider the self at a particular moment as a separate, isolated individual is to consider an abstraction. The self is an integrated unity embracing both its past and its environment. The self, as it proceeds through time, grows with the past duration it accumulates; hence its past is gathered up into and contained snowball fashion within it. In this sense it is or rather it includes its past Karma which cannot be effaced. The environment is only an aspect of a unity, a whole, of which the individual is himself the other aspect; thus the mode in which the self is conditioned by its environment is, like the mode in which it is conditioned by its past, a mode of self-conditioning.

Now it is precisely this integrated self which, as we have seen, is the vehicle of an indwelling spirit, and, the more integrated, the more effectively a vehicle. This spirit, which is continuous with God, which, indeed, is God, is free. It is free in two senses; first, within the limits of the framework imposed by past Karma it is free to choose its actions, as the bridge player, although his play is conditioned by his cards, is nevertheless free to choose one card rather than another. It is free, secondly, in the sense that the individual can in the last resort liquidate his accumulations of Karma, and emancipate himself entirely from the trammels of the past.

But while he has freedom, it is not the freedom

to do just what he pleases. The self-determinism of past Karma stretching from the past into the present effectively precludes the irresponsibility of caprice. "Freedom is not caprice since we carry our past with us. The character at any given point is the condensation of our previous history. What we have been enters into the 'me' which is now active and choosing. . . . The past can never be cancelled, though it may be utilized."[1]

Thus the determination exercised by the past is a matter of degree. It is the spirit in man that is free, and this freedom becomes actualized to the extent to which his personality becomes actualized, that is to say, becomes integrated. The more integrated the personality, the greater its freedom of choice; but in the case of every human being, however inchoate, there is a potential freedom of which he can always in theory avail himself. A man may be almost exhaustively analysable, as Kant would say, from the point of view of anthropology, almost completely a cork bobbing on the waves of instinct and desire; but he is never quite; and, in so far as he is "not quite," it will always be true of him that "he can" because "he ought."

ST. THOMAS AQUINAS ON FREEDOM

One of the best treatments of the subject of human freedom with which I am acquainted is that of St. Thomas Aquinas; it also seems to me to express very well the attitude which underlies

[1] *An Idealist View of Life*, p. 278.

Radhakrishnan's own doctrine. The great difficulty in the conception of freedom is, as St. Thomas sees, that choice is never without a motive, the motive, let us say, to have A rather than B, and the motive may determine, and often is said to determine, the choice. How, then, can the choice be free? The essence of St. Thomas's account is that while I am deliberating between A and B, making a comparison of their respective "goodnesses" on which my act of choice will depend, there is a definite stage of indecision, a period in which I am "indetermined to either alternative." When the comparison is finished and the estimate 'A is better than B' is made, the period of indetermination is over; my will is now *determined*—determined, that is, to take A and leave B, and what it is determined by is my own judgment of their relative worths. Now in making this judgment it is admitted that I shall be influenced by all the factors upon which modern psychology lays stress, by the violence of present desires, the persistence of prejudice, the effects of past habits, the drive of unconscious impulses and, as Plato insists, the bias arising from the sum-total of my choices in the past. Nor is it contended that it is easy to eliminate the influence of all these factors. But what are necessary as the minimum conditions of freedom of choice are the admissions first, that the elimination is sometimes achieved, that we do sometimes make an *impartial* comparative judgment of the relative worths of two goods of which we cannot have both, and, what is more, choose in accordance with our judgment;

and, secondly, that what is achieved sometimes can in theory be achieved always.

DEPENDENCE ON METAPHYSICAL VIEW

Can the admissions be made? I think that they can, but only if we are prepared to accept a metaphysical hypothesis such as that of Radhakrishnan, which insists that the ultimate reality not only of man but of the universe is spirit, which as it manifests itself in and in relation to human beings is a free, a changing, a developing spirit. This, it will be remembered, was the teaching of the last chapter. Restating it in terms of this one, we may say that, since spirit is the reality of the universe, freedom is the reality of man. And it is of course the case that, unless we are prepared to accept Radhakrishnan's metaphysical background or some metaphysic approximating to it, our statement is in effect a begging of the question. In this sense Radhakrishnan's ethics, and particularly his teaching on freedom, stand or fall with his metaphysics.

Grant the background, and he is entitled to say in the words with which I sum up his doctrine: "The human agent is free. He is not the plaything of fate or driftwood on the tide of uncontrolled events. He can actively mould the future instead of passively suffering the past. The past may become either an opportunity or an obstacle. Everything depends on what we make of it and not what it makes of us. Life is not bound to move in a specific direction. Life is a growth and a growth is undetermined in a measure. Though the future is the sequel of the past, we cannot say what it will be. If there is no indetermination, then human consciousness is an unnecessary luxury."[1]

[1] *An Idealist View of Life*, p. 279.

CHAPTER VI

PENDANT ON IMMORTALITY

INTRODUCTORY

The object of conduct, I quoted in the last chapter from Radhakrishnan's *Indian Philosophy*, should be a continuous "discipline of human nature leading to a realization of the spiritual."[1] Proceeding to discuss the duties of man, his freedom and the continuance of his personality through a plurality of lives, I omitted from the discussion any mention of the object, the "realization of the spiritual," to which the whole process of training and discipline enjoined by Hindu ethics is directed. Ethics, I pointed out, is for Radhakrishnan the handmaid of religion; we are exhorted to live in a certain way in order the more fully to enjoy religious experience. It is this conception of religious experience as the end of life, or rather of lives, that remains to be worked out. The elaboration of the theme will involve a discussion of Radhakrishnan's views on immortality and of his distinctive conception of social immortality.

AN OBJECTION

The discussion may best be introduced by way of an objection to Radhakrishnan's ethical scheme, which he states and answers in *The Hindu View of Life*. Let us suppose that we waive the difficulty

[1] *Indian Philosophy*, Vol. I, p. 41.

raised in the fourth chapter constituted by the need for a further principle, a medium other than God in which God's creation could take shape and assume, as on Radhakrishnan's view we are bound to do, that everything is in some sense the Absolute and that everything that *we know* is in some sense God. Are not rules of life, then, unnecessary, since the evils against which they are designed to guard us are unreal? Why, in fact, bother with ethics at all? The question expresses a point of view which is frequently urged against Hindu thought: "To the Hindu ethical rules are meaningless because the world is divine. Everything is God, and there is no excuse for our interfering with the sacred activities of the pickpocket or the perjurer."[1] Radhakrishnan holds that this difficulty arises from a faulty conception of God's relation to the world. It is true that God is immanent in the world, and that He is, therefore, present in some degree in everything. But the presence *is in fact* one of degree; He is more fully present in some things than in others: "While there is nothing which is not lit by God, God is more fully revealed in the organic than in the inorganic, more in the conscious than in the unconscious, more in man than in the lower creatures, more in the good man than in the evil. . . . While Hinduism believes in the divine indwelling and declares that there is no escaping from the divine presence, it does not say that everything is God as we find it. Piccadilly is not God, though even Piccadilly cannot be unless it is allowed by divine activity."[2]

[1] *The Hindu View of Life*, p. 70.   [2] Ibid., p. 71.

It is difficult to avoid the reflection that, if there are degrees in the presence of that which is God, there must also be degrees in the presence of that which is not. The less X is God, the more X is something that is not God. What? It is hard to say. Granted the existence of something in the universe that is neither God nor the Absolute, an intractable subject-matter in which God manifests Himself with greater or less fullness, and this particular difficulty disappears. But this is again to introduce the further principle which Radhakrishnan will not admit; it is to impair the unity of his Monism by the introduction of a 'something other'; it is, in fact, to postulate a duality.

We must leave the difficulty and proceed to develop the ethical implication of Radhakrishnan's position, which is that, if God can be present in varying degrees, it is our duty to increase the degree of His presence, to enable Him to realize Himself more fully in us and, in so doing, to realize more fully ourselves. The object of evolution, in fact, both in us as individuals and in the species as a whole, is so to evolve that the potentially divine in us may become actual.

THE CONDITIONS AND CHARACTERISTICS OF SELF-REALIZATION

When this consummation is reached we achieve immortality; we also achieve divinity. What are the marks of this condition? First, by meditation and quiet, by contemplation and discipline, the individual has achieved unity with himself. He has become a completely integrated personality. Already we have intimations of this condition in mystical experience. The intuitive apprehension of the mystic is an activity in which, as we have seen, instinct and intellect are fused and transcended. Moreover, there are human beings, biological 'sports' as it were, in whom this spiritual capacity for direct mystical experience is developed beyond the level normally reached in their fellow-men. The spiritual genius, as Radhakrishnan calls the mystic, is a harbinger of the future, a signpost pointing along the road which all may and all one day will travel. In his moments of insight he has already achieved heaven, heaven being not a place but simply a state of realizing our full possibilities: "Heaven and hell are states of the self and not places of resort."[1] "These geniuses from whose quivering lips ecstatic utterances leap up, give us a foretaste of what all human beings are destined to be. They are the heralds of the infinite, the first-fruits of the future man. They and the moods of exaltation they rouse in us are a promise of mankind's future achievement in spiritual understanding. They are the new 'emergents,' the beginnings of a new human species."[2]

Thus the doctrine of evolution is invoked to give ground for the hope that, just as life at the amoeba stage became life at the reptile stage, just as the

[1] *An Idealist View of Life*, p. 294.
[2] Ibid., p. 209.

reptiles evolved into the mammals, the mammals produced the lemur, the lemur was insensibly transformed into the human being, so "the human being may become divine."[1] Again, in this application of the theory of evolution we see how Radhakrishnan makes use of concepts derived from Western science in the development of a traditional Eastern doctrine. When divinity is reached, finality is reached; there is no more rebirth, for rebirth is subject to time and is inevitable only "so long as we stick to the individualistic position. If we transcend individualism, we rise superior to the phenomena of time and thus escape from rebirth. . . . To seek for liberation from the wheel of births and deaths is nothing more than to rise to the spiritual level from the merely ethical."[2] And the condition so realized is not merely a life like the present purified and spiritualized and extended *ad infinitum*. It is "a new mode of being, a transfigured life here and now."[2] For "the spiritual is not" merely "the extension of the ethical. It is a new dimension altogether, dealing with things eternal."[2] It is "a new creation in the order of the universe . . . not a mere unfolding of the human."[2]

But for its realization a further condition must be satisfied. The individual must be integrated not only with himself but with his environment, that is, with other individuals; and this second integration cannot be achieved so long as any single, individual

[1] *An Idealist View of Life*, p. 210.
[2] Ibid., p. 304.

self remains unrealized. Thus we come to Radha-krishnan's distinctive conception of social salvation.

SOCIAL SALVATION

The end of religion is, as we have seen, the realiza-tion of the potentially divine in man; such realization means that the self, in becoming itself, becomes also the God which is immanent in the self, becomes, therefore, perfect. But this state of perfection cannot be realized by the individual alone, if only because the individual cannot, as we have seen, be divorced from his environment. If to consider him so divorced is to consider him as he is not, it follows that his nature is infected through and through by the environment of which he forms part. Unless, therefore, the environment, in so far as it consists of other individual souls, also achieves perfection, he cannot himself be perfect. Perfection, in fact, is a state of the whole, not of any single part: "In a true sense the ideal individual and the perfect community arise together."[1] Thus it is the duty of each individual to seek for salvation not only for himself but also for his neighbours. This social salvation, which is the ultimate aim of life, is the achievement of a community of fully realized spirits: "If one human soul fails to reach its divine destiny, to that extent the universe is a failure."[2] But "if the infinite love of God is not a myth, uni-versal salvation is a certainty."[2]

[1] *An Idealist View of Life*, p. 307.
[2] *The Hindu View of Life*, p. 125.

It is, then, the duty of the 'saved' to help those who are not yet 'saved.' Radhakrishnan insists on the duty of those who have achieved harmony with themselves to assist those who have not: "Those who have secured a vision of spirit work in the world so long as there is wrong to be set right, error to be converted and ugliness to be banished from life. The individual who achieves unity within himself sets other men forward in desiring the same good."[1]

In view of this obligation to assist in the salvation of the world, the fully realized individual does not throw off his individuality. Nevertheless the perpetuation of individuality is not the end of life. The Christian conception of the preparation for eternal bliss of a number of human souls conceived in the likeness of twentieth-century Nordic adults as the purpose for which creation travails, seems childish to the Hindu. The view is, it is obvious, a figment born of the pride of over-developed individuality, arising in the minds of those who, unable to contemplate the extinction of their own personalities with equanimity, cling frenziedly to self. Hinduism has no particular attachment to individuality or desire to perpetuate it. Nevertheless the conception of social salvation requires that "so long as some individuals are unredeemed, the other freed souls have work to do and so retain their individuality."[2]

[1] *An Idealist View of Life*, p. 307.
[2] Ibid., p. 310.

THE NATURE OF IMMORTALITY

Radhakrishnan rejects personal immortality. We cannot, he points out, conceive of ourselves as individuals and yet existing endlessly. For what sort of individuals should we be? "We do not want endless youth, or endless old age. Whatever it be, if it is endlessly continued, we will be sick unto death."[1] He also rejects the notion of 'conditional immortality,' the view that some only will be saved and that salvation depends upon behaviour. The Christian view that "immortality is not our natural birthright . . . but a prize to be won"[2] overlooks the facts first, that a man has many lives in which he can repair the errors of this one, that to leave any eternally unsaved argues God a devil, and that, as we have seen, none can achieve perfection until all do. The notion of eternal damnation, moreover, is as childish as that of eternal, individual bliss; however bad a man may be, we must suppose (again unless God is a devil) that in future lives he will improve, and improve continuously: "God's patience is not likely to be exhausted in the short span of a single life."[3] We can only infer that "all individuals are destined to gain life eternal."[4]

The ultimate end is one in which individuals achieve unity not only with God but with one another, "by a perfect interpenetration of mind by mind."[4] Until that consummation is reached, saved

[1] *An Idealist View of Life*, p. 282.   [2] Ibid., p. 283.
[3] Ibid., p. 286.   [4] Ibid., p. 307.

souls, although at the moment of their release from Karma they achieve a universality of spirit, nevertheless retain individuality "as a centre of action as long as the cosmic process continues."[1] The object of this retention is to enable them to assist in the redemption of other souls; the necessity for it arises, as we have seen, from the fact that "harmony with the environment is not possible so long as there are unredeemed elements in it."[2]

THE END OF THE WORLD PROCESS

The end of the whole world process is emancipation from the process. It shall be described here in Radhakrishnan's own words.

"It cannot be that certain individuals will remain for all time unredeemed. If they are all redeemed, it cannot be that they sit down in heaven, praising God and doing nothing. So long as some individuals are unredeemed, the other freed souls have work to do and so retain their individualities. But when the world as such is saved, when all are freed and nothing remains to be done, the time process comes to an end. The threats of science that the world will be wound up one day need not depress us. The universe though 'unbounded' is 'finite.' The end of time may mean the perfection of humanity, when the earth will be full of the knowledge of spirit. The cosmic purpose is consummated so far as the conditions of space and time

[1] *An Idealist View of Life*, p. 306.
[2] Ibid., p. 307.

allow."[1] Ultimately, then, all individuals achieve immortality in God. When this happens, "the end of the plot is reached. Earth and heaven would be no more; the timeless and the transcendent alone remain."[2]

The object of the world process is, therefore, the achievement of a state of universal and changeless perfection. God, as we saw in the fourth chapter, falls back into and is merged in the Absolute; all individual souls, as we have recounted in this one, fall back into and are merged in God.

The menace disclosed by science that oppresses the West, the menace of the destruction of life on this planet when the sun collides with another star or burns itself out, is, for Radhakrishnan, a figment born of our obsession with matter and the material. Once realize that life is not dependent on matter, that matter, indeed, is only an illusion of the spirit, and the possibility of the end of life may be dismissed by the Western philosopher—at least, it may be, if he can bring himself to accept the view of an ultimate submergence of all life in the static perfection of the Absolute which Radhakrishnan puts before him. Nirvana is the end, evolution is the method, God the mediator and guide, so far as this world plot is concerned. Thus Radhakrishnan fuses and reconciles three strains of thought, Oriental mysticism, scientific evolution and Christian personalism.

[1] *An Idealist View of Life*, p. 310.
[2] Ibid., p. 309.

CHAPTER VII

RELIGION IN THE MODERN WORLD

RELIGION NOT RELIGIONS

Radhakrishnan is a deeply religious man, widely known for his exposition of a fundamentally spiritual view of the universe, a universe in which God is passionately affirmed. I, on the other hand, am an avowed agnostic, openly critical of official religions, author of a book, *The Present and Future of Religion*, wherein official Christianity as preached by the Anglican Churches and embodied in their organization is repudiated, and its continued decline prophesied and acclaimed.

When I referred to this obvious divergence of outlook, Radhakrishnan assured me that the differences between us were only superficial. I believed with him that the familiar world of daily life did not exhaust the universe, that spirit was a reality, matter not the only type of existent; I held, too, as he did, that values were real, and that the advance of the human spirit was to be measured by reference to its increasing capacity to apprehend them. So much was common ground between us. But there was, he pointed out, a closer bond, closer and more immediately relevant. It was not so much that I with him held that in *some sense* the religious view of the universe might be ultimately not indefensible; it was much more that he with me held that religions were the chief deterrent to its accept-ance. Religion, but not religions, is what, in his view, the world needs. Just as the spiritual view of the universe has no more eloquent advocate, so the dogmas in which the religions have formularized the vision of man's spirit, the bonds in which they have confined it, the deeds and creeds and codes and rubrics in which they have inscribed it, docketed it, tied it up in bundles of red tape, and pigeon-holed it, and the claims to exclusive truth, the assertions of unique revelation by which they have proceeded to justify themselves for imposing their forms and demanding acceptance for their formulae, have no more bitter critic. "Nothing," he writes, "is so hostile to religion as other religions."[1] "The world would be a much more religious place if all the religions were removed from it."[1]

This antagonism to religious forms and creeds runs like a recurrent motif throughout his thought, appearing in the most unexpected places. He holds, for example, that religious partialities and partisan-ships are responsible for what he regards as the chaos of Western philosophy.

CRITICISM OF WESTERN PHILOSOPHY

One of his earliest books, *The Reign of Religion in Contemporary Philosophy*, is devoted to an expo-sition of this thesis. Radhakrishnan, as we have seen, is an Absolute Idealist, who holds that the universe is a spiritual unity. Much modern philosophy is

[1] *An Idealist View of Life*, pp. 44, 45.

realist and pluralist; it holds that the world contains many different and ultimately different things, and that spirit, even if irreducible and ultimate, is not exhaustive; it is one element in a world that owns others. This Pluralism Radhakrishnan believes, and, in this book, seeks to show, is due to the intrusion into philosophy of considerations proper to religion. Western philosophers are not, he holds, impartial; they use philosophy as an instrument to support pre-formed religious convictions.

"It is my opinion that systems which play the game of philosophy squarely and fairly, with freedom from presuppositions and religious neutrality, naturally end in absolute idealism; and if they lead to other conclusions, we may always suspect that the game has not been played according to the rules. The current pluralistic systems are the outcome of the interference of religious prejudice with the genuine spirit of speculation."[1]

I have not space here to follow the argument of this highly original book. Radhakrishnan considers one by one the leading systems of Western philosophy, those of James Ward, of Bergson, of Bertrand Russell, of the Pragmatists, and seeks to show not only how in deviating from the Absolute Idealism they deviate from truth, but that the deviation is due to unacknowledged religious presuppositions. For my part I find this conclusion surprising. Many pluralists are to my own knowledge thoroughgoing agnostics, nor should I in general agree that the

[1] *The Reign of Religion in Contemporary Philosophy*, p. vii.

pluralist and realist trends of Western philosophy are due to religious prejudice. But what I want to stress is the antagonistic attitude to current religions which is so pervasive a feature of Radhakrishnan's thought. It is this antagonism and its consequence which will form the subject of this chapter.

I. Radhakrishnan's Interpretation of Hinduism

The first and immediate consequence is the presentation of the religion of Hinduism as a model religion, a model religion just because it is not in the strict sense of the word a religion at all. In matters of belief it is neither detailed, definite nor positive. Insisting on conduct rather than creed, it is not fanatical, does not proselytize, and, while it lays no claim to exclusive revelation for itself, is respectful of the revelations of others.

In *The Hindu View of Life* Radhakrishnan gives unstinted praise to the spirit which has traditionally animated the beliefs and practices of Hinduism. I select three features of that spirit which he specially commends, as an appropriate introduction to Radhakrishnan's view of the position and function of religion in the modern world with which this chapter will be mainly concerned.

1. THE ACCEPTANCE OF ALL

In the first place, Hinduism is tolerant of different creeds. In *The Hindu View of Life* Radhakrishnan emphasizes the number of invaders who have at various times descended upon India; each new wave of primitives brought with them their own special habits, ways of life and religious beliefs. Three methods of dealing with the invaders were open to the comparatively civilized inhabitants of the Indian peninsula: extermination, subordination and integration. Extermination is a mode of behaviour which is repugnant to the civilized intelligence; it is only the young and the primitive who feel the wish to destroy something because it is strange. "Hello! There's something different. Let's hit it," while expressive of an attitude all too common in the West, is not the natural reaction of the cultivated Hindu. Subordination means enslavement and subjection. A subordinated people gradually loses its distinctive way of life; either it is absorbed and becomes indistinguishable from the ruling race, or its mentality degenerates into that of a servile and subject class.

Now Hinduism proceeds from the assumption that every people has its unique contribution to make to the wisdom, understanding, thought and culture of our race. A people may be primitive and elementary; it may be too young in development to have produced an original art, evolved a native culture, or exhibited any distinctive grace of mind or creativity of spirit. Nevertheless, it is impossible to say what potential stores of understanding, skill, creativity and enlightenment it may one day contribute to the common human stock. But, if the contribution is to be made, the people must be allowed to develop along its own lines. Its spiritual growth must be neither suppressed nor distorted. A democracy, a community of equals, in which each grows to his full stature through intercourse with others, and in which each by contributing something which is uniquely his own contributes to the growth of all—such is the ideal which the Hindu method of integration seeks to realize.

In pursuance of this method each group in the heterogeneous racial complex which is the people of India has been allowed to develop to the full its own individual potentialities. Hinduism is like a vast reservoir into which each successive race of newcomers has poured its vivifying stream of primitive freshness and vigour. Continuously strengthened and vitalized by these infusions, Hinduism has in its turn enriched the newcomers from its stores of traditional culture. As with the peoples, so with their beliefs: "Hinduism developed an attitude of comprehensive charity instead of a fanatic faith in an inflexible creed. It accepted the multiplicity of aboriginal gods and others which originated most of them outside the Aryan tradition, and justified them all."[1]

Hence Hinduism developed from the first a wide tolerance. "Hinduism is wholly free from the strange obsession of the Semitic faiths," an obsession which Christianity has so regrettably inherited "that the acceptance of a particular religious metaphysic is necessary for salvation, and non-acceptance thereof

[1] *The Hindu View of Life*, p. 37.

is a heinous sin meriting eternal punishment in hell.''[1] Hindus do not proselytize; they do not lay *exclusive* claims to salvation, and they do not believe that God will be pleased by the wholesale slaughter of those of His creatures whose beliefs are mistaken. As a result Hinduism has been less disgraced than most religions by the anomaly of creed wars. Buddha's followers have not shown their respect for their master's injunction to love their neighbours by roasting, racking and disembowelling them in his name, and the history of Hinduism holds no parallel to the horrors of the Inquisition or the Thirty Years' War.

RELIGION A SYMBOL OF THE UNKNOWN

Radhakrishnan's own theology is imbued to the full with this traditional Hindu tolerance. We have seen how he regards religious beliefs, as he regards scientific theories, in the light of symbols under which we represent to ourselves a reality essentially unknowable. But, if one holds that a religious doctrine is a convenient symbol and not an absolute truth, it is difficult not to concede to others the right to employ the symbolization that each finds most appropriate. "The intellectual representations of the religious mystery are relative and symbolic. As Plato would say, our accounts of God are likely stories, but, all the same, legendary. . . . We are like little children on the seashore trying to fill our shells with water from the sea."[2] But "while we

[1] *The Hindu View of Life*, p. 37.   [2] Ibid., p. 36.

cannot exhaust the water of the deep by means of our shells, every drop that we attempt to gather into our tiny shells is a part of the authentic waters."[1]

2. THE UNIQUE CONTRIBUTION OF EACH

But just because no religion has final value, every religion has some. Every creed has some truth to offer, even if no creed has The Truth. Given toleration, the fact of the diversity of religious creeds should not occasion regret. Granted the Hindu view of religion, which seeks its unity "not in a common creed but in a common quest,"[2] then "the world would be a . . . poorer thing, one if creed absorbed the rest. God wills a rich harmony not a colourless uniformity."[3] We are enjoined, then, to welcome varieties of belief, provided that none lays claim to exclusiveness, in order to justify hostility to some rival exclusiveness. The more complex the voices that enter into a Fugue, the better the Fugue; the more diverse the facts that are integrated in a whole, the richer the whole. What is important in forms of belief as in forms of life, in creeds as in organisms, is that each should be allowed to grow to its full stature, to realize all that it has in it to be, to become completely itself.

Here, then, is a ground for the respect which a higher culture may justly extend to a lower. Granted that the lower is a good thing of its kind, granted that it completely realizes itself, then, though the

[1] *The Hindu View of Life*, p. 36.
[2] Ibid., p. 58.   [3] Ibid., p. 59.

kind be humble, it will nevertheless have value and deserve respect. As the *Bhagavad Gītā* has it, "Better is one's own *dharma*" (duty and development on one's own lines) "though destitute of merit, than the well-executed duty of another." This does not mean that a savage should remain and be content to remain at a level "destitute of merit"; merely that he should become a perfect savage instead of an imitation civilized man.

This familiar Aristotelean conception that every-thing has its own good, the good appropriate to its kind, continually reappears in Radhakrishnan's thought. We are not—the law of Karma forbids it—free to be the sort of beings we should wish; we may not select our race, our country, our parents, our talents, our circumstances, even our vocation. But we can make the best of our heredity and our circumstances. "Freedom," in fact, "consists in making the best of what we have, our parentage, our physical nature and mental gifts."[1] Moreover, "every kind of capacity, every form of vocation, if rightly used, will lead us to the centre."[1]

The more and the more different kinds of developed individuals it incorporates, the richer the community which incorporates them. Hence "the task of the civilized is to respect and foster the live impulses of backward communities and not destroy them. Society is an organism of different grades. . . . Every type has its own nature which should be followed. No one can be at the same time a perfect saint, a

[1] *The Hindu View of Life*, pp. 126, 127.

perfect artist and a perfect philosopher."[1] Just as
every individual has his own contribution to make
to the life and thought of society, each according to
his kind, so every society has its contribution to
make to the life and thought of the species. And
just as each individual has his own unique insight
into the nature of things, his own mode of recognizing
the reality that draws and excites him, and his own
mode of expressing in art and conduct his individual
recognition of it, so no less has each nation. The
genius of one people is different from another;
inevitably, then, its culture and beliefs will be different. "Each nation has had its own share of the
inner light and spiritual discovery. No cultural and
religious imperialist who has the settled conviction
that he alone has all the light and others are groping
in darkness can be a safe guide in comparative
studies. It is not fair to God or man to assume that
one people are the chosen of God, their religion
occupies a central place in the religious development
of mankind, and that all the others should borrow
from them or suffer spiritual destitution."[2] Moreover,
"each group has its own historic tradition, and
assimilation of it is the condition of its growth of
spirit."[3] Hence "the Hindu method of religious
reform . . . allows each group to get to the truth
through its own tradition by means of discipline of
mind and morals."[3] The creeds of men, in fact,
are different the world over, although the spirit

[1] *The Hindu View of Life*, p. 127.
[2] Ibid., pp. 50, 51.   [3] Ibid., p. 42.

which leads men to formulate them is the same in all. Just as it takes all sorts to make a world, so does it take all sorts of minds to make the truth about the world.

APPLICATION TO PHILOSOPHIES AND PHILOSOPHERS

Spiritual truth, as we have seen, is revealed to the intuitive insight of individuals; but the revelation is only partial. Moreover, directly the recipients of the vision seek to communicate it, they blur, misreport and fall into error. Philosophy, which is the organized communication of spiritual truth, inevitably botches its message in transit. This is not a reason for discarding philosophy; it is a recognition of the fact that, while all philosophies contain some truth, all contain, and inevitably, a degree of error. The progressive development of philosophy consists in the progressive reduction of the error and, in consequence, of the progressive enlargement of the truth. It is easy to show where philosophical systems are wrong, harder to show where they are right. Yet it is in their rightness and not in their wrongness that their value consists. On examination their common deficiency will be found to consist in adopting some conception valid in itself, and then illegitimately expanding it to embrace the universe. Philosophers, in other words, have mistaken partial truths for whole ones. In *The Reign of Religion in Contemporary Philosophy* Radhakrishnan seeks to show in regard to the various systems dominant in contemporary Western thought that each suffers from this same error, the error of illegitimate extension of concepts, of treating, that is to say, some valid but partial principle of interpretation as if it constituted an account of the whole.

In a final chapter he offers certain suggestions of his own, suggestions which were subsequently to appear as a fully fledged system in the *An Idealist View of Life*. His method, he avers, is suggested by that of the Upaniṣads, according to which "the pursuit of truth is more negative than positive, more an escape to incomplete conceptions than the attainment of perfect truth. . . . By an immanent criticism of conceptions, we are enabled to discover the most complete, or the most fundamental idea, relatively to the rest."[1] Philosophy consists, in fact, of a continual pooling and sifting of the conceptions of philosophers. The more diverse the conceptions, the richer the material to be sifted. None is to be rejected, because, while none is true, none is wholly false.

THE DUTY OF TOLERANCE

As with philosophy, so with religion. We none of us possess exclusive insight or ultimate truth; what alternative, then, have we but to welcome the insight of all, to treat with respect the convictions of all? Again and again in this connection Radhakrishnan inveighs against the intolerance and exclusiveness of religious sects and their leaders. Paraphrasing

[1] *The Reign of Religion in Contemporary Philosophy*, pp. 413, 414.

Fielding's parson Thwackum, he says: "Those who love their sects more than truth end by loving themselves more than their sects. We start by claiming that Christianity is the only true religion and then affirm that Protestantism is the only true sect of Christianity, Episcopalianism the only true Protestantism, the High Church the only true Episcopal Protestant Christian religion, and our particular standpoint the only true representation of the High Church view."[1]

The reproof applies with terrible appropriateness to the sectaries of the West. Enlightened by a supposed exclusive revelation men have tortured and killed one another in hundreds and thousands in the endeavour to make them share the interpretation which they have seen fit to found upon it. That the Holy Ghost proceeded from the Father and the Son, or that He proceeded from the Father only, that bread and wine are or are not body and blood, or that in some mysterious sense they both are and are not at the same time, are propositions in defence of which men have killed one another in thousands, and practised hideous tortures upon thousands. Yet none of these propositions can be known to be true, and it is exceedingly improbable that absolute truth resides in any of them. The enthusiasms of fanatics have written some of the darkest pages of human history. The commands of Christ who bade His followers love one another have been so perverted by the mistaken zeal of His adherents that the

[1] *The Hindu View of Life*, p. 51.

gospel of love and peace has become mankind's favourite excuse for hatred and violence; while His obstinate refusal to identify right with might has served as a pretext for the view that the best way to prove the truth of your convictions is to go on hurting people, until they consent to share them. It is small wonder that to-day sensitive Westerners turn in disgust from a religion which has been responsible for some of the most infamous cruelties that have disgraced the records of our kind. Religion, if it is to regain a hold upon the affections of men, must adopt a better way, the way of tolerance for conflicting views, of respect for diverse revelations: "The Hindu theory that every human being, every group and every nation has an individuality worthy of reverence is slowly gaining ground."[1] Possibly; possibly not. Radhakrishnan's words were, of course, written before the Nazi terror in Germany. Meanwhile, it is permissible to point out that it is in a world of religion which, while incorporating the creeds of all, nevertheless transcends them that the hope for the future lies. "The Hindu spirit is that attitude towards life which regards the endless variety of the visible and temporal world as sustained and supported by the invisible and external spirit."[2] The spirit, in other words, is one. The expressions of the spirit will be as various as there are human beings. Very well, then, let us respect them all!

[1] *The Hindu View of Life*, p. 51.
[2] Ibid., p. 124.

3. THE RELIGION FOR MODERNS AND FOR SCIENCE

The attitude just summarized is not only consonant with the modern scientific spirit; it is the only one which can be made tolerable in a world increasingly imbued with the spirit and the standards of the man of science. Comparing Bergson with Radhakrishnan, Professor Muirhead writes: "What if in the religion which is being expounded, with certain doctrinal differences but with a singular unity of spirit, by two writers who occupy similar positions as leaders of thought in Europe and in India, we have just the vital faith for which they both think the world is waiting—one which, instead of dividing continents and sects within them, is capable of uniting them in a single allegiance, not to any material crown or empire, but to the values which are the crown of life and the empire of the spirit."[1] Of this spirit, of these standards certain characteristics may be predicated.

THE SCIENTIFIC TEMPER

(a) THE RELATIVITY OF TRUTH

In the first place, science is impatient of dogmatism. For the typical declaration of dogmatic religion, "Thus saith the Lord," it substitutes the comparatively humble announcement, "the evidence is on the whole not incompatible with the assertion that." Science, in a word, is not committed to the assertion

[1] *Hibbert Journal*, October 1932.

of absolute truths; it is interested less in the establishment of truth than in the formulation of hypotheses, hypotheses increasingly validated or gradually revised, if the evidence demands revision. Science is thus tentative in statement and provisional in conclusion where religion has been certain and absolute. It follows that the scientist, unlike the theologian or the priest, is willing to withdraw his assertions and to modify his conclusions. The road which science has travelled is littered with the debris of the theories which scientists have discarded, 'phlogiston' and homunculi packed up in spermatozoa, the Newtonian theory of force and the doctrine of fixed types. Under the influence of science the West has come to distrust absolutes of all kinds. It is imbued with the conviction that truth is provisional and relative; that it ought to be continually open to review and that no barrier of dogma should be allowed to impede the process of its revision. This scepticism in regard to our possession of absolute truth is a necessary outcome of the rapidity with which new knowledge has been obtained. The modern universe is more mysterious and elusive than the world of the nineteenth century. The area of what is known being diminished, the field of what is possible is correspondingly enlarged. Not only is there scepticism as to the conclusions reached, but doubt as to the proper methods of reaching them. Hence men are not only more willing to explore different avenues of possible understanding of the universe, art as well as science, religious ecstasy as well as common sense, but within the boundaries of science itself they are continually trying new instruments. As Sir William Bragg says, "We use the classical theory on Mondays, Wednesdays and Fridays, and the quantum theory on Tuesdays, Thursdays and Saturdays." This scientific temper dominates men's minds as never before. It characterizes our age as completely as the instinctive acceptance of dogmas characterized the age of faith. In the dry, critical atmosphere that science engenders the notion that religion can give us absolute and detailed truth about the universe seems crude and primitive, even at times a little vulgar, and by educated people is regarded with contemptuous amusement. To adopt a vivid phrase from Walter Lippmann's *A Preface to Morals*, "the acids of modernity" have not only proved corrosive of the traditional account of the supernatural government of the universe; they are likely to eat no less destructively into the substance of any substitute accounts that are likely to be provided.

(b) THE DEMAND FOR EVIDENCE

In the second place, the scientific habit of mind insists on demanding evidence for beliefs. Its conception of what constitutes evidence is admittedly apt to be a little narrow; it is apt also to extend the demand to spheres in which it cannot be complied with: for example, to those of aesthetic appreciation and religious experience. What evidence, for example, can there be for the view that Shakespeare is a better playwright than Webster, or Mozart a better musician than Rossini, except such as is afforded by the feelings of their readers and hearers? But these being private cannot be offered for inspection and comparison, just as the works of art which arouse them being qualitatively and not merely quantitatively different cannot be assessed by the methods of quantitative measurement. And so science is a little apt to dismiss the spheres of art and religion as merely subjective, or was so until recently. Of recent years, with the abandonment of materialism, a change has set in. The imaginative conception of reality no longer being limited by what we can see and touch, other avenues for the exploration of the universe are beginning to be envisaged, other forms of evidence than those which science has been accustomed to recognize in the past to be admitted. That intuition may, for example, carry the assurance of its own certitude is, as we have already seen, coming to be fairly widely conceded. But the assurance is unfortunately incommunicable. So is the evidence for religious truth. Very well, then, even if we are no longer to write off, as we were once inclined to write off, religious revelation as a figment, because it cannot give an account of itself when called to the bar of scientific verification, we shall be at least able to decide between the merits of different revelations. If we no longer look upon all religions as the expression of man's childish passion for certitude, which prompts him to supply the place of ignorance by converting his conjectures into dogmas, we shall still be suspicious of the dogmas. At best they are, we hold, symbols of a reality which they indicate rather than describe, and between the different indications there is, as far as we can see, no method of deciding. So the modern Westerner, applying what he conceives to be the modern scientific attitude to the claims of religion.

What follows? First, that while religion as such may be valid, no single religion can be wholly true; equally, however, it need not be wholly false. Secondly, that for this reason we must be tolerant, respectful even, to all religions. But this is precisely the Hindu attitude to which we may now return.

HINDUISM AND THE DEMANDS OF SCIENCE

Science, Radhakrishnan holds, is hostile to the dogmas of religion, not to its spirit. "Religion as revelation or dogma has no appeal to the believer in science,"[1] for "the scientific temper is opposed to the acceptance of dogma."[1] Science, in fact, "has no sympathy with . . . *a priori* schemes of revealed religion."[1] That there must be a God because the ontological proof demonstrates the necessity, that He must be beneficent because reason—but is it, indeed, reason and not emotion?—will not have it otherwise, that the world is His creation, that the world is, therefore, good and evil is a mere appearance, such deductive affirmations from *a priori* principles leave the scientific mind unmoved. The scientific mind approaches religion in a scientific

[1] *The Religion we Need,* pp. 10, 11.

spirit. Its method is impersonal and inductive; "it starts not so much with the creator as with the creation. It studies the facts of nature and society and frames an idea of God to suit them."[1]

And, inevitably, it recognizes that the idea is not a truth but an hypothesis, to be tested by its working and judged by its ability to square with the evidence. A religious belief is, therefore, for the scientist not a dogma directly revealed by God, but a conception evolved by man, faulty, anthropomorphic, provisional and, like all man-made concepts, liable to revision

Radhakrishnan, interpreting Hinduism, is in complete agreement. "The idea of God is an interpretation of experience."[2] "The creeds of religion correspond to the theories of science."[2]—I have already quoted in the second chapter this vivid phrase in which Radhakrishnan crystallizes his attitude to religion and scientific truth.

Hence our third conclusion is this. Because it is tolerant to all, because it welcomes the unique contribution of each, because it recognizes truth in all but absolute truth in none, the Hindu attitude to religion is that which is peculiarly congenial to, is, in fact, alone compatible with the temper of science. Western science, provisional, empirical and undogmatic, and Hindu religion, tolerant, hospitable and undogmatic—between these two, says Radhakrishnan, there is a natural although unrecognized

[1] *The Religion we Need*, p. 11.
[2] *An Idealist View of Life*, p. 86.

affinity. Of that affinity he is the spokesman. Between these two there is a bridge; across it he moves to and fro, the natural interpreter of each to the other. And here we pass from his interpretation of the traditional spirit of Hinduism to the exposition of his own personal views, which that spirit has informed.

II. Religion and the Unity of the World

THE PRESENT WORLD SITUATION

Science, it is a commonplace, has made the world economically a single unit. The nations are members one with another in so intimate a sense that the poverty and insecurity of one are quickly found to be the poverty and insecurity of all. In this interdependence, which should be the greatest good, lies the greatest danger of our time. For, though economically one, the world is politically a congeries of nationalist states consumed by *sacred egoisms*, each insisting on its territorial integrity, each proclaiming its inalienable sovereignty, and each at the moment seeking to shelter from the economic blizzard behind high tariff walls which intensify the very distresses from which all are suffering. At the moment of writing every nation is trying to sell to all and to buy from none, with the result that men and women throughout the world go cold and hungry for want of those very things whose surfeit is ruining the producers who are unable to dispose of them. The world, in a word, is going to ruin through the inability of its producers to get rid of the goods for which the would-be consumers are starving because of their inability to buy.

For this paradox the root cause is, as I pointed out in the Prologue, a disparity between our scientific technique and our social wisdom such that the latter is quite incapable of devising a mode of distributing the goods so abundantly produced by the former. Our social wisdom is still conditioned by the ideas of the past; it is informed by a narrow parochialism. Nation and class are the blinkers between which we look out upon the world, and, because of them, most of us are incapable of thinking in terms of world citizenship or of humanity as a whole. One of the most notable expressions of this mentality at the moment is the policy of economic nationalism. Each nation, in trying to score off its neighbours to the advantage of itself, contributes to a situation in which each is being rapidly ruined by the activities of all. Our statesmen and business men are dominated by a fundamentally nationalist outlook. To a world which is economically one, they apply the sectional policies of competing hostile units, and try to solve problems which are world wide alike in incidence and origin, in terms of the traditional concepts of the Foreign Office and the parish pump. Until this mentality is changed, until these jealous national states which see everything in terms of nation, nothing in terms of humanity are superseded, until, in a word, the world develops an international mind commensurate with its international structure, there is no escape from our present difficulties. Sooner or later, if they persist, they will wreck our civilization.

RELIGION AND THE NEED FOR A WORLD OUTLOOK

In the diagnosis of the situation just given Radhakrishnan fundamentally concurs. The progress of science has, he points out, changed material conditions too fast for the adaptive capacity of the human mind. The conditions for a world civilization exist; indeed they are such that only a world civilization is compatible with them. Only the minds of men are unprepared: "The products of spirit and intelligence, the positive sciences, the engineering techniques, the governmental forms, the legal regulations, the administrative arrangements, and the economic institutions are binding together peoples of varied culture and bringing them into closer reciprocal contact. The world to-day is tending to function as one organism."[1] But "though humanity has assumed a uniform outer body, it is still without a single animating spirit. The world is not of one mind";[2] "the outer uniformity, in fact, has not resulted in an inner unity of mind and spirit."[3]

Nothing short of a new political synthesis can meet the needs of the times, a political synthesis which is rooted in a new world outlook. How is that outlook to be born? Radhakrishnan's answer is that it can be born only in religion.

[1] *Kalki*, p. 9.   [2] Ibid., p. 10.   [3] Ibid., p. 9.

Before we trace in detail the development of this answer, let us examine its relevance to the immediate situation. Granted that, as Radhakrishnan insists, mankind is a single organism, it must have a single goal. As Dante proclaimed, there is not "one goal for this civilization and one for that, but for the civilization of all mankind there is a single goal." This goal is to be sought not in uniformity but in harmony. What, on this view, is needful, is not a common culture, but an harmonious blend of different cultures; of different cultures and of different creeds. Here, then, once again, we meet the Hindu concept of truth in all, exclusive truth in none in a new setting. The religions of the world can only live together, if they are tolerant of each other; what is more, by virtue of such tolerance religion may become a force not for the dividing of mankind but for its binding. If Radhakrishnan's metaphysic is right, it is the same spirit which informs each of us, and religion is nothing but its development and realization; it is also the development and realization of the true self. In realizing ourselves, then, we realize also our kinship with one another through the common spirit that binds us. This, then, is Radhakrishnan's call to religion, a call to give to this generation a common spiritual outlook, as science has given it a common material framework.

CAN MAN AVOID DESTRUCTION?

I have presented this common spiritual outlook as if it were a good, which humanity must seek to achieve, if it is to advance. I might with equal justice have represented it as a condition which must be satisfied if humanity is to survive. The next war—it is a commonplace—will destroy our civilization. That war is inevitable unless nations can be induced to abandon their claims to absolute national sovereignty and to submit to the jurisdiction of an international sovereignty vested in a League of Nations, I take to be self-evident. Civilized man has proceeded for hundreds of years on the assumption that each nation is entitled to be judge and jury in its own cause, with the result that, whenever a nation has wanted anything or feared anything badly enough, it has preferred to risk the hazard of war rather than to trust to the arbitrament of neutrals to decide its claim. And to risk the hazard of war has meant in practice that the only method which you were prepared to admit to determine the justice of your cause was to kill off as many members of the opposed nation as you possibly could. The nation which showed a superior efficiency in slaughter to its enemy regarded itself as having mysteriously demonstrated its superior morality. These are the methods of the jungle, and they have brought Western civilization to the verge of destruction. If I may repeat a phrase from the Prologue, it is not necessary to show that mankind is worse than it ever was to demonstrate the urgency of the danger; merely that it has a need to be better, since, as I proceeded to point out, the new technique which science has placed at its disposal has so dangerously increased its effectiveness in destruction. When a lunatic is unarmed, his quarrelsomeness is merely a nuisance; if he possesses a revolver, he becomes a public danger. Mankind to-day has become so dangerous to itself that the nations of the world have no alternative but to learn to behave better, if they want to avoid destruction.

To learn to behave better means in the present context to be willing to submit causes of dispute to an international authority and to abide by its decision. Such a willingness implies, as I have already pointed out, a change of mind; indeed, it depends upon it, since in the present state of national sensitiveness peoples feel that their honour is impugned unless they are allowed to implement their views by killing their opponents. So long as men think in terms of national honour, the danger will remain. The need of the times is, then, for an international outlook, which thinks in terms of humanity, civilization or the world. Can religion help in generating this new outlook? Radhakrishnan, as we have seen, thinks that it can. On what lines does he substantiate his view?

THE POLITICAL FUNCTION OF RELIGION

His political ideal for the world "is not so much a single empire with a homogeneous civilization and a single communal will, but a brotherhood of free nations differing profoundly in life and mind, habits and institutions, existing side by side in peace and order, harmony and co-operation, and each contributing to the world its own unique and specific best, which is irreducible to the terms of the others. The cosmopolitanism of the eighteenth century and the nationalism of the nineteenth are combined in our ideals of a world-commonwealth, which allows every branch of the human family to find freedom, security and self-realization in the larger life of mankind."[1]

The ideal of a world commonwealth may be assisted, it may even be conditioned by that of a world religion. Just as the rivalries of warring creeds have been a potent cause of war in the past, so their blending in an harmonious recognition of the spiritual reality of the world may be as potent a cause of peace. But, the fact is obvious, the claim to exclusiveness must be given up if the blend is to be achieved. "When two or three different systems claim that they contain the revelation of the very core and centre of truth and the acceptance of it is the exclusive pathway to heaven, conflicts are inevitable. In such conflicts one religion will not allow others to steal a march over it, and no one can gain ascendancy until the world is reduced to dust and ashes. To obliterate every other religion than one's own is a sort of bolshevism in religion which we must try to prevent."[1]

And, again, we are pointed to the Hindu solution, which in the striking phrase I have already quoted "seeks the unity of religion not in a common creed but in a common quest."[1] It is on these lines that Radhakrishnan would look for an alleviation of the

[1] *The Hindu View of Life*, p. 58.

present world discontents. Science has given the world material unity; we need a spiritual unity to match it. The challenge to mankind to-day is to establish a political harmony born of a uniform outlook on the world, just as it has established a uniform environment of material conditions. That political harmony cannot be, until men are willing to regard themselves as citizens of the world, considering the world's problems as their own, not citizens of a nation, considering the difficulties of every other nation the advantage of their own. How is this new political outlook to be generated? It can only arise as the outcome of a new spiritual orientation, which welcoming the diversity of creeds by which men have sought to express their relation to the unseen world, refuses to find the complete truth in any. Each creed must bring its individual contribution to man's understanding of the spiritual world, and of his purpose and function as a part of the spiritual world, just as each nation must bring its individual cultural contribution to the harmonious government of the political world. It is in this sense that religious idealism seems to Radhakrishnan "to be the most hopeful political instrument for peace which the world has ever seen."[1]

If it is to perform this function, religion must be comprehensive, "embracing within its scope all those who are religious-minded in sentiment, allowing them full liberty so far as creeds and thought-

[1] *Kalki*, p. 96.

pictures are concerned"[1]; it must be "not so much a theory of the supernatural as an attitude of spirit, a temper of mind."[1] As to belief, it is enough that the "religious-minded in sentiment" should subscribe to the "central dogma of all true religion," which "is the possible perfection of man, his inherent divinity, and the invincible solidarity of all living beings with each other in the life of God."[2] Man cannot, in fact, Radhakrishnan would seem to suggest, be religious-minded, unless he subscribes to this dogma. Such is the religion which the world demands to-day; such, if our civilization is to survive, must be the religion of the future.

NECESSITY OF DIVERSITY IN CULTURE AND CREED

A unified religion, which implies no more than a world-wide assent to the "central dogma" of religion, does not necessitate, nor should it, a barren uniformity either of conduct or of creed. For—and the insistence on the status of both religion and science as symbols of the unknown may have obscured the point—unity does not mean uniformity. Individual differences are to be welcomed and blended not transcended. Science, or rather human beings misusing the fruits of science, have, as we saw in the Prologue, established a civilization whose dull uniformity has robbed life of the grace of variety, and ironed out the irregularities in which the charm of individuality consists. Man has drilled himself into uniformity by his subservience to machines,

[1] *Kalki*, p. 60.   [2] Ibid., p. 68.

which have imposed something of their soullessness upon those who serve them. He has misused these new powers of coal and steam, petrol, electricity and ferro-concrete with which science has invested him to stamp out his own individuality. All over the world man comes increasingly to resemble man. A journey from Burslem to Basra does not to-day present the traveller with the varieties of sight and sound, of culture and environment with which it would have delighted him a hundred years ago. To this extent it brings less of enrichment and refreshment to the spirit. It is good that there should be differences between race and race, culture and culture, and that the human spirit should express itself in an infinite variety of ways: "God wills a rich harmony, not a colourless uniformity."[1]

RELIGION AND DAILY LIFE

Finally, Radhakrishnan insists, religion is essential to the life of the individual, essential, that is, if the business of living is to be made tolerable. Whether or no we share Radhakrishnan's metaphysical view of his nature and origin, man, we must concede, is, at least in part, spirit. Unless we are to hold the view that this generation consists almost exclusively of biological 'sports,' and that its psychological make-up accordingly omits an element which all previous generations of mankind have included, we must suppose that this spiritual element is still present in the contemporary Western Nordic. Yet, as I pointed

[1] *The Hindu View of Life*, p. 59.

out in the Prologue, it is denied adequate outlet. It can give no assent to the supernatural asseverations of the primitive creed in which it has been nurtured, while, as the recent war showed, it has no assurance when the testing-time comes that this creed will in any way affect the conduct of those who profess it. On the contrary. . . .

No substitute set of beliefs seems likely to take the place of those we have outgrown. Hence men's spiritual faculties tend to atrophy through lack of organized occasions for their expression. It is difficult to avoid the conclusion that men and women to-day suffer from a suppression of their spiritual impulse, as marked and as deleterious as that suppression of the sexual impulse which they have been taught by the psycho-analysts to regard as so pitiable a deficiency in their fathers.

The inference is obvious; we are as undeveloped spiritually as we are over-developed intellectually. It is to this fundamental disparity between intellect and spirit that the lopsidedness of our civilization to which I referred in the Prologue, the lopsidedness born of the disparity between our scientific skill and power over nature on the one hand and our social wisdom on the other, must be attributed. To it the fundamental unliveableness of life as it presents itself to many of our contemporaries[1] must be, at least, in part ascribed.

[1] See, for example, M. André Malraux's *Les Conquérants,* or almost any novel by Aldous Huxley in England, or Theodore Dreiser in America.

INADEQUACY OF HUMANISM

When a crisis comes, a world war or a world economic collapse, men who have traditionally found in religion refreshment for the spirit, solace for suffering and strength to meet the emergency, find that they have nowhere to turn. A barren humanism is their resource, but humanism, which may serve well enough in normal times, is pitiably inadequate in times of stress. Intellect can criticize and exhibit as illusory the consolations of religion, but it can offer no alternative solace from its own resources: "When the foundations of life are shaken, when the ultimate issues face us demanding an answer, humanism does not suffice. Life is a great gift, and we have to bring to it a great mood; only humanism does not induce it."[1] Yet, at the moment, we have no alternative to humanism. Why not? Radhakrishnan gives the answer at which we have already hinted; it is because our spiritual development lags so far behind our intellectual: We have now "the assertion of mind over life and matter: and yet not of spirit over mind, life and body."[2]

This is the theme round which *Kalki* is written. It sets before us an ideal of civilization, an ideal in which the spirit is developed concurrently with the mind, until the present disastrous separation between them is transcended in an harmonious blend: "Unless the mind is interpreted as one with spirit,

[1] *An Idealist View of Life*, p. 69.
[2] *Kalki*, p. 47.

we have not reached the ideal of civilization."[1] But it is not enough for mind to become one with spirit. The unity which is both must become one with the world spirit which, immanent in all of us, is yet, as we have seen, the ultimate reality of the universe. "It is the transformation of the individual into the universal outlook, the linking up of our daily life with the eternal purpose that makes us truly human."[2]

IMPORTANCE OF VALUE

The theme is not a new one. Man, Radhakrishnan insists again and again, becomes fully himself by becoming one with reality. How is this oneness to be achieved? An unregenerate child of my age and civilization, I do not know. Nor in the last resort can Radhakrishnan tell me: "Each must tread the weary mountain from the top of which alone the vision can be seen in all its splendour. The teacher may put us on the way, speak to us of the hazards and hardships, but grasping the final mystery is an individual achievement."[3]

But that this fullness of being to which Radhakrishnan's exhortations, informed by the secular wisdom of the East, summon us is in some way bound up with value, that a civilization which lacks value and a sense of value cannot stand (has not Radhakrishnan himself drawn attention to the toughness in terms of survival value of the Eastern civilizations, their

[1] *Kalki*, p. 40.   [2] Ibid., p. 43.
[3] *An Idealist View of Life*, p. 121.

triumphant emergence from oppression and conquest, their supreme long-livedness compared with the formidably armed and armoured civilizations of the West, and asking from whence this long-livedness is derived, answered that the lively awareness of value on the part both of individuals and communities confers precisely that toughness of fibre which characterizes the spiritual life of the East?) and that it is in its demand for a renaissance of value and a sense of value that the gist of Radhakrishnan's message to the West is to be found, these things, I think, I know. And, that I may end as I began on a note of personal comment and exposition, I add a short epilogue on the lack of value in the contemporary West, and upon its consequences as we observe them in the world around us and recognize them in our own lives. I began by anticipating, I end by applying what I take to be Radhakrishnan's message to the West in the light of my own philosophy and experience.

THE NEED OF THE WEST

This Epilogue seeks to present in a brief compass a picture of a civilization which, having lost its sense of values, is palpably incommoded by the lack.

PURE AND IMPURE PLEASURES

The charge that Radhakrishnan brings against us may be stated in a number of ways. Plato in the *Philebus* makes a celebrated distinction between pure and impure pleasures. Impure pleasures are those which depend upon a preceding state of want, of need, of pain. Thus the pleasure of the convalescent is determined by and relative to the cessation of the illness from which he has been suffering; when we have been in pain, the mere discontinuance is felt as pleasant. Necessarily related to wanting, to needing, to suffering, impure pleasures may be said to include as an integral part of themselves some element of that to which they owe their origin. Again, impure pleasures cannot persist, since the condition upon which their pleasantness depends, the "unpleasure" from which they spring, quickly fades from memory. The pleasures which consist in the satisfaction of appetite, the pleasures of food or of sex fall pre-eminently within this category.

The enjoyment of a pure pleasure on the other hand owes none of its pleasantness to any condition other than itself. The pleasures we take in music, in art, in the acquirement of knowledge, in the exercise of our faculties, or in the enjoyment of the country-side are not conditioned by preceding want or pain. We do not have first to be miserable, we do not even need to feel desire or to be conscious of a lack, in order to enjoy the sparkling brightness of a frosty morning. For this reason pure pleasures may be prolonged—prolonged and indefinitely repeated. In the enjoyment of pure pleasures appetite, which is quickly sated with the impure, grows with what it feeds on. Thus the artist and the countryman grow to love art and the countryside better as they know them better, not less. Pure pleasures must not, however, be pursued for the sake of their pleasantness. We should not go into the country to obtain pleasure but because we want to visit the country. Thus the disappointment which so often attends the attempt to repeat a pleasure arises from the fact that on the second occasion we pursue for its pleasantness something which on the first we sought for itself. This last reflection, however, opens a side road down which I must not venture. So with a recommendation to the reader, especially if he be modern, to consult the tenth Book of Aristotle's *Ethics*, where the nature of pleasure is discussed with an almost final adequacy, I turn to Schopenhauer.

SCHOPENHAUER ON OVERPLUS OF PAIN

Schopenhauer affirmed as the underlying principle of life an unconscious urge or impulse which he called the Will. Every individual organism is, for Schopen-hauer, a particular manifestation of the Will. The Will expresses itself in the individual in a continuous series of wants or needs, and the pain of want causes him to take action designed to satisfy the want. When the want is satisfied, he feels pleasure, but only for a moment, since, as want or desire is the essence of life, the satisfied want is immediately replaced by another. Hence pleasure, which attends the satisfaction of want, is dependent on the pre-existence of the want which it satisfies. We cannot, therefore, obtain the pleasure of satisfaction without undergoing the preceding pain of want, and the attempt to enjoy the pleasure after the want is satisfied results only in boredom and satiety. It is for this reason that the devotees of the life of so-called pleasure, which consists in the attempt to enjoy continuous pleasure without experiencing the intervening pain of want, are traditionally the most, not the least dissatisfied of human beings. Since the pain of need or desire is a permanent condition of living and the pleasure of satisfaction is transitory, life, according to Schopenhauer, regarded as a com-mercial speculation with pleasure on the profit and pain on the debit side, is doomed to bankruptcy.

Again, if needing or wanting is the permanent condition of living, satisfying one want will be merely a preliminary to experiencing another. We cannot remain satisfied, try as we will, but are driven for-ward by the remorseless urge of life, to make ever fresh efforts to achieve satisfaction. This according to the argument is bound to be short-lived, while pain is certain and continuing. The obvious conclusion is that, the sooner we cease to exist, the better for us.

Schopenhauer, the fact is alas too clear, was a pessimist. The effect of his pessimism is to obliterate Plato's distinction between pure and impure pleasures, and to relegate all pleasures to the category of the impure. Schopenhauer may be right, but it seems unlikely. The lives of hundreds of thousands of reasonably happy people refute him. There are ways of living—the way of the craftsman who loves his work, of the moderately good artist who achieves recognition, of the scientist who devotes himself to the discovery of truth, of the woman who, happily married, produces and brings up loved and creditable children—in which, the evidence seems overwhelming, the balance between pleasures and pains inclines clearly to the credit side of the account. Making, therefore, our bow to this hypothesis, alleged, although as far as I can see unjustly, to be supported by the practice and theory of the East, we come to a typical modern Western philosopher, Bertrand Russell.

CREATIVE AND POSSESSIVE IMPULSES

In his *Principles of Social Reconstruction*, Russell distinguishes between creative and possessive impulses. The distinction, we are expressly warned, is made for purposes of convenience; it is not invested with ultimate metaphysical or even psychological validity. "Some of our activities," says Russell, "are directed to creating what would not otherwise exist, others are directed towards acquiring or retaining what exists already. The typical creative impulse is that of the artist; the typical possessive impulse is that of property." Now the best life "is that in which creative impulses play the largest part and possessive impulses the smallest."[1] Russell's theory, it is obvious, invokes a standard of value. The creative impulses, he urges, should be encouraged at the expense of the possessive. And for an obvious reason. The creative impulses can be encouraged and indulged to an unlimited extent without interfering with the impulses of others. When the creative impulse of the artist produces a picture, the result does not impede the production of other artists, but rather acts as a stimulus to activity, by challenging their emulation. The possessive impulse, however, which leads a man to acquire and retain a large fortune can only be gratified by the deprivation of others.

Creative impulses issue as a rule in the production of things which may be enjoyed by an indefinite number of people. A symphony or a poem is like the air, the country, or the sea in this, that the fact of its being enjoyed by others is no obstacle to its enjoyment by oneself. The possessive impulses, on the other hand, instead of increasing the possibilities of enjoyment, limit them by confining them to the possessor and his friends. It is easy to see how the indulgence of the possessive impulses leads to strife

[1] Russell, *Principles of Social Reconstruction*, p. 234.

and conflict, whereas the creative impulses of many, even, perhaps, of all, may be harmoniously developed without friction.

Now the structure of modern society is such as to encourage the expression of the possessive impulses to the almost complete exclusion of the creative. We in the West live under a system which, though paying lip service to the religion of Christ, who waged unceasing war upon the possessive impulses—"Take no thought for your life, what ye shall eat, or what ye shall drink; nor yet for your body, what ye shall put on"—creates a scale of values which counts only in terms of the satisfaction of the possessive impulses, by making income and property the chief criteria of importance and success. The impulses that demand beauty and spaciousness and leisure, spaciousness for romance and leisure for creation, are brushed aside as incompatible with the all-important business of 'getting on,' which being interpreted means the acquisition of the means for increasing our material possessions.

The possessive impulses are not a direct expression of the principle of growth; they are the outcome of what is static and conservative in human nature rather than of what is dynamic and changing. In those who are old the possessive impulses have achieved on almost complete victory over their inconvenient creative brethren, and it is for this reason that our institutions, which are the embodiment and expression of the ideals of the old, aim at perpetuating possession by setting upon it the seal of security and respectability. The supreme principle both in politics and in private life should, according to Russell, be "to promote all that is creative, and so to diminish the impulses and desires that centre round possession."[1]

THE AVOCATIONS OF THE RIVIERA

Russell's analysis endorses from another angle the pleas of Plato and of Schopenhauer; we should aim at pure rather than at impure pleasures; we should not directly seek pleasure at all; we should express creative rather than possessive impulses. Now let us take a look at the pursuits of a society which is founded upon a negation of these doctrines. You will find them most clearly exhibited to the eye of dispassionate observation on the Riviera, where you will also find an industry that exists for the sole purpose of providing with amusements those who cannot amuse themselves. Those engaged in this industry proceed on the supposition that the temperament of rich and idle persons is equivalent to that of small and spoilt children. Since, however, they are in years adults, a circumstance which makes it impracticable to force them to do things by beating them, and, since in order to escape the demon of boredom, they must nevertheless do things, the object of this industry is to create in them the impression that they are discovering interesting and important things to do for themselves. It is a fundamental principle among those engaged in

[1] Russell, *Principles of Social Reconstruction*, p. 236.

inventing occupations for the rich to discover for themselves that they can never stand any amusement for more than an hour. Before the hour is over they become bored, and, like spoilt children tiring of their toys, must be amused with something else. They spend an hour in sun-bathing, an hour at a motor rally, an hour at polo, an hour at cocktails and reading the papers in the sun. The theatre thoughtfully provides long intervals so that people may gamble as a relief from watching the play, and there is dancing as a relief from gambling. They have a particular penchant on the Riviera for shooting half-blinded pigeons.

IDEALS OF WESTERN MAN

The Riviera scene manifests in an extreme form the symptoms of the disease of Western civilization. The form is extreme only because the favoured few, whose combined wealth and leisure enable them to devote all their energies to the cultivation of the ideals of their civilization, express in concrete actuality what in most of us remains a latent yearning. For who can doubt that the working and middle classes of the Western world, endowed with the same opportunities, would utilize them in the same way? Inevitably, since they are dominated by essentially the same conception of the good life. To hit balls with pieces of wood, or to kick them with leather boots, or more frequently to watch other people hitting and kicking them; to kill birds and animals, to amble slowly over glazed floors to the strains of negro music, to lunch in London and dine in Paris—these for the average Westerner constitute the pursuits of the good life. A life which embodied them uninterruptedly would, he considers, be perfect.

These admired pursuits are informed by three main ideals. First, the ideal of the rapid movement of pieces of matter from one place to another, depending, where the piece of matter concerned is the human body, upon the implied belief that any place is better than that in which it happens to be; secondly, the ideal of the acquisition of the greatest possible number of material objects, known as possessions; thirdly, the ideal of entertainment, that is, of paying other people to perform for us the office which we can no longer perform for ourselves.

Each of these ideals and the pursuits to which they prompt us can be shown on analysis to be self-stultifying. They carry with them, as Hegel would say, the seeds of inherent contradiction. They can neither be maximized nor universalized. Each on examination reveals the ground of its own self-stultification. Consider, for example, our use of leisure.

MACHINES, LEISURE, TRAVEL, SOLITUDE

The purpose of machines is, it is obvious, to provide man with leisure; in fact, they do not do so, man, who has invented machines to serve him, having become so enslaved to his servants through his own lazy dependence upon them that he has never worked so hard in tending his fellow-men as he works to-day in tending machines.

But let us grant that the machines gave man leisure. What use is he to make of it? To the working, still more to the overworking, man, leisure is undoubtedly a good; but beyond a certain point freedom from work produces a diminishing return of happiness. Those who are completely freed hasten to commit themselves to a merciless round of pleasure in order to escape from the intolerable task of providing themselves with reasonable occupation; they worship that gloomiest of deities, the god of "a good time." Now, servitude to the need for amusement is, as the Riviera sketch suggests, the most exacting of all the forms of slavery to which human beings have yet subjected themselves. It is significant that the suicide rate among the unemployed rich is the highest of any class in the community.

As it is with leisure, so it is with travel. Lauded as a means of relieving the monotony of the unemployed Westerner's existence, travelling, excessively pursued, becomes self-stultifying. Travelling is praised because, in bringing the traveller into contact with new peoples and scenes, curious customs, strange creeds and alien cultures, it diversifies and enriches his personality; but, if travelling becomes sufficiently universal, no curious customs, no alien cultures will be left. There was a point in travelling from London to Madrid, or even to Leeds, when the culture of Madrid was different from that of London;

when even in Leeds there survived North Country idiosyncrasies which gave the Southerner that mingled sense of insecurity and distinction wherein the charm of travelling lies. But, as men and women move increasingly from place to place, the world becomes increasingly one place; local peculiarities die out and the same standard civilization of the film, the radio, the cocktail, the motor and the jazz-band meet him everywhere.

The solitude of nature is again commended as a source of strength and refreshment for the jaded spirit; but the more the people who seek it, the more difficult it becomes to find, while Nature herself, ravished by the embraces of her too numerous lovers, loses her power either to solace or to charm. Those who love the country, as the fate of the English countryside is only too effectively demonstrating, quickly find that they have no country left to love. Instances could be multiplied indefinitely of the truth of Schopenhauer's strictures as applied to the life which consists in the search for distraction. Yet of the life of effort and endeavour there seems no reason to suppose them true.

HAPPINESS IN EFFORT

The secret of happiness, if we are to believe the traditional wisdom of the sages, is to be found in the continual exercise of the faculties in arduous endeavour upon an appropriate subject-matter; it consists, in fact, in not having enough leisure to wonder whether you are miserable or not. So far

R

as the life of the body is concerned, many in the
contemporary West have come to realize the fact,
and, having learned by experience that no game is
worth playing, unless it is played as if the winning
of it were the only thing in the whole world that
mattered, young Westerners of the middle classes
subject their bodies to discipline and training as a
preliminary to undergoing the ardours and endur-
ances of the running track or the football field. It
is the subconscious realization of the same truth
that sends men mountain climbing, exploring or
big-game shooting. These men escape the boredom
that waits upon the pleasure-seeker, and enjoy the
happiness which comes to all who struggle. But
theirs is not the greatest happiness of which man
is capable, because the struggle takes place on a
lower level than the highest at which life has now
manifested itself.

It is not for lack of effort that the average
Westerner is to be censured, but for lack of effort
of the right kind. Effort, if it is to satisfy, must be
the effort of the highest of the faculties and capaci-
ties which human beings have evolved; it must, in
other words, be effort of the mind and of the spirit,
not of the body. That effort in the world of thought
can be as exciting as effort in the world of matter
is a truth which the average Westerner fails to
realize. Yet life, it is obvious, has now evolved at
a level at which such effort alone is permanently
satisfying, so that, just as the urge of life once
drove men to acquire new qualities of physical

skill and to lay up fresh reserves of physical endur-
ance in the struggle against nature, so it now finds
its most appropriate expression in the effort to
paint a picture or to remodel a social system, to
realize life imaginatively in fiction or to grapple
with the problems of abstract thought. Thinking is
now the appropriate activity of normal, educated
men, just as the apprehension of objects of value
in artistic creation and mystical contemplation is
the privilege of the race's most advanced representatives. In all ages men who have had the opportunity
to try every kind of life, combined with the energy
and talents to give the more exacting lives a fair
trial, have seemed to reach agreement on this one
point, that the only things which can give permanent
satisfaction are the employment of our highest
faculties at maximum intensity, alternating with the
recreation of the mind in music and art and literature and the conversation of one's friends. Such, at
least, has been the worldly teaching of the sages.

RECOMMENDATION TO THE INTELLIGENT HEDONIST

The doctrine of effort and activity that I have
sketched is pre-eminently, did he but know it, the
doctrine for the intelligent Hedonist. It alone on
the balance sheet of life can give a credit of pleasure
over boredom. Throw yourself body and soul into
your work, lose yourself in an interest, devote yourself to a cause, lift yourself out of the selfish little
pit of vanity and desire which is the self by giving
yourself to something greater than the self, and on

looking back you will find that you have been happy. Nor, if I read Radhakrishnan aright, is the doctrine so much at variance with the teaching of the greatest of Hindus of the past, which is also the teaching of one of the greatest minds of the contemporary West. "The teaching of history," writes Mr. Wells in the *Outline of History*, ". . . is strictly in accordance with the teaching of Buddha. There is, as we are seeing, no social order, no security, no peace or happiness, no righteous leadership or kingship, unless men lose themselves in something greater than themselves. The study of biological progress again reveals exactly the same process; the merging of the narrow globe of the individual experience in a wider being. To forget oneself in greater interests is to escape from a prison." The truth is one which many have preached. Devotion to impersonal ends offers the only way of escape from a fatal self-absorption. Through it alone can we forget the nervous little clod of wants and ailments which is the self, by losing ourselves in something bigger than the self.

INTRODUCTION OF VALUE INTO THE ARGUMENT

To this doctrine, which I have put forward as a purely worldly one, a doctrine to be commended to the calculating Hedonist, Radhakrishnan gives a spiritual backing. If you want to be happy in this life, I have said, lose yourselves in something greater than the self. If you want to save your soul in this and the next life, he adds, do likewise.

Radhakrishnan, in fact, would supplement my worldly doctrine with the exhortation to cultivate the life of the spirit. Is there in modern Western man no chord which will vibrate responsively to his appeal? I have already hinted in this book at the renaissance of the philosophy of value in the West. Here, in a few sentences, is my own phrasing of its content.[1] The universe contains as real and independent factors objects of value, of which the most eminent, so far as the human mind can discern, are truth, goodness and beauty. Apprehended by man's mind, these are nevertheless other than his knowledge of them. Yet by most of us these values are not apprehended directly, but only when they are manifested[2] in a sensuous medium. Life, in fact, has not yet evolved at a level at which it is capable of a direct vision of value. We see its reflections only in the material medium of which we are made aware by our senses. Hence we apprehend beauty in pictures and music, goodness in actions and dispositions. Even so, moreover, our vision is fleeting and intermittent; we cannot prolong aesthetic pleasure any more than we can continuously enjoy moral feelings, so that in aesthetic enjoyment we obtain fleeting glimpses rather than a full view of the Beauty that moves us. Nor should we succeed

[1] A full statement will be found in my *Philosophical Aspects of Modern Science*, Part II.

[2] I use the word "manifested" loosely. The question of the precise relationship between objects of value and material things and actions which are recognized as possessing value raises highly controversial issues.

in obtaining even these fleeting glimpses, were it not for the assistance we derive from the artist.

FUNCTION OF THE ARTIST

In common language we may say that the artist detects the manifestation of beauty in that which the ordinary man sees only as an object of everyday use. So long as his vision lasts, the artist remains rapt in contemplation, thrilled to ecstasy by the image of the real which has been vouchsafed to him. But, as I have already pointed out,[1] the vision does not last. Life is a dynamic, changing force, an ever-restless surge, which, though it may ultimately come to rest in the untrammelled contemplation of the world of value, has not yet emerged at a stage at which such contemplation is either possible or desirable. The most that has yet been vouchsafed even to its favoured children is a fleeting and intermittent glimpse. The veil is lifted only to be redrawn. While aesthetic contemplation lasts, we are will-less and self-less, but only for the moment. Scarcely is he assured of the unique character of what his vision reveals before the artist is caught up again into the stream of life, and pulled back into the world of need and want, of struggle and desire, to which his status as an instrument of life's will inevitably condemns him. But, before his memory fades, he enshrines his vision in paint or sound or song. Hence a work of art, as I have suggested in Chapter II, is a souvenir which the artist makes to

[1] See Chapter II, pp. 86, 87.

remind him of a reality which he has known and knows no longer. Art is thus the window through which life gets its first intimation of the nature of the world of value; its function is, to use a metaphor of Plato's, to turn the eye of the soul round to reality, by revealing the element of significant form in virtue of which the things of the material world show forth the patterns of the world of value which underlies them. Yet it is not beauty itself that the artist contemplates, but only its image in a material setting; only the mystic may contemplate beauty and truth directly, and even he, as Radhakrishnan assures us, cannot retain his vision for long.

CONCLUSION

Radhakrishnan's interpretation of the universe goes, as we have seen, far beyond what is here suggested. For these objects of value which the traditional culture of the West enjoins us to pursue are, he holds, nothing less than aspects ot the supreme value which is the spiritual reality of the universe. Moreover, this supreme value, in its aspect of personal god, is the very spirit in man by the light of which he also perceives it. Thus Radhakrishnan invokes the religious insight of the East to give a spiritual background to the recommendations of the worldly wisdom of the West. Taking the intimations of our aesthetic experience, he interprets them in the light of a religious experience which transcends our vision and of a spiritual theory of the universe which outstrips our thought.

To grant his claim is to grant the authority of spiritual insight to sanction principles reached in the West by experimental methods of worldly trial and error. Radhakrishnan confirms, in a word, by the light of the spirit the practical ethic which we in the West have hammered out by the experimental methods of science. Here, then, is the most notable of the bridges that he is seeking to build between East and West.

BIBLIOGRAPHY

OF WORKS BY RADHAKRISHNAN

The Philosophy of Rabindranath Tagore (Macmillan, 1919).

The Reign of Religion in Contemporary Philosophy (Macmillan, 1920).

The Philosophy of the Upanisads. Foreword by Rabindranath Tagore. Introduction by Edmond Holmes (Allen & Unwin, 1924).

Indian Philosophy, 2 vols. (Allen & Unwin, 1923. Library of Philosophy. Revised edition, 1929).

The Hindu View of Life (Upton Lectures, Allen & Unwin, 1927. Third impression, 1931).

The Religion We Need (Benn, 1928).

Kalki, or the Future of Civilization (Kegan Paul, 1929).

An Idealist View of Life (Hibbert Lectures, Allen & Unwin, 1932).

INDEX

GEORGE ALLEN & UNWIN LTD
LONDON: 40 MUSEUM STREET, W.C.1
CAPE TOWN: 73 ST. GEORGE'S STREET
SYDNEY, N.S.W.: WYNYARD SQUARE
TORONTO: 91 WELLINGTON STREET, WEST
WELLINGTON, N.Z.: 8 KINGS CRESCENT, LOWER HUTT

Outlines of Indian Philosophy

by M. HIRIYANNA, M.A.

Formerly Professor of Sanskrit, Maharaja's College, Mysore

Demy 8vo.   15s.

"So lucid and thorough . . . that it deserves to be used as a text book in colleges where Indian philosophy is taught."—*Sheffield Daily Independent*

The Six Ways of Knowing

Demy 8vo.   by D. M. DATTA   15s.

This volume gives a comprehensive and clear survey of the principles of Indian Logic, with due references to the corresponding features in Occidental Logic. It appeals, therefore, both to students of Indian thought in itself and to those who are interested in its affiliations to more familiar systems, while the specific characteristics of the subject are duly emphasized.

"A critical study of the Vedanta theory of knowledge, and a thorough piece of work by competent hands . . . lucidity of statement and real helpfulness in revealing the working of the Indian mind."—*Expository Times*

A Study in Æsthetics

by LOUIS ARNAUD REID, Ph.D.

Independent Lecturer on Philosophy in the University of Liverpool

Demy 8vo.   15s.

Both artists and critics are concerned, in very different ways, with æsthetic principles. In this work the author examines and criticizes the ideas—explicit and implicit—involved in the production and appreciation of æsthetic objects. Among the many topics discussed are "expression"; "beauty" and "ugliness"; "functional" beauty; artistic production and motivation; "greatness," "perfection" and the problem of varying standards of these; the relation of art to truth, to reality and to moral values; the competition of interests in arts like opera; the tragic, the comic, the classic and the romantic. The book concludes with a chapter on "The Enigma of Natural Beauty."

"This spirit of frankness and facing the facts gives Dr. Reid's views on a difficult subject special significance."—*Public Opinion*

The Fundamentals of Ethics

Demy 8vo.   by WILBUR MARSHALL URBAN   12s. 6d.

"A brilliant and interesting manual, noteworthy for its balanced judgment and for the acuteness of its literary illustrations."—*Times Literary Supplement*

The Death of Materialism
by W. WHATELY CARINGTON
Demy 8vo. (WHATELY SMITH) 10s. 6d.

The author approaches the problems of Materialism and of the anti-thesis of Mind and Matter from an unusual angle.

Although, in his early chapters, he discusses the psychological factors which commonly promote misconceptions on the subject and indicates why the arguments usually adduced in favour of Materialism are necessarily inconclusive or invalid, he is primarily concerned to show that the problems in question are false and non-existent, being artificially created by our acceptance at their face value of verbal formulations which are actually no more than Fictions—provisional constructs of a certain practical value but unfit for retention at an advanced level of discourse.

From the fields of Psychical Research and of orthodox Psychology certain phenomena are selected as demanding a revision of the ordinary conceptions of Personality and indicating that of a Universal Conscious-ness of which individual minds are but localized offshoots. This con-ception, it is claimed, leads to conclusions in striking conformity with mystical experience and enables us, in principle at least, to unify the realms of the Mystical and the Rational.

"A whole-hearted, spirited and immensely amusing attack on the philosophical materialist."—*New Statesman*

The Essence of Plato's Philosophy
by CONSTANTINE RITTER
Demy 8vo. TRANSLATED BY PROF. ALLES 16s.

The author of this outstanding volume has gained a world-wide reputa-tion as an authority on Plato, to whose life and philosophy he has devoted his career. Professor Ritter enjoys the distinction of being the only thinker specially mentioned in Professor A. E. Taylor's Dedication to his own well-known work in this field. The entire trans-lation has been undertaken with the view to presenting Professor Ritter's orginal conclusions clearly and concisely, so that all readers who are interested in the subject can follow the development of the themes dealt with. The philosophy of Plato is not merely one of the greatest and earliest systems in the long history of thought, but it will ever retain its deep influence on all speculation on knowledge and ethics, on social ideals and international organisation. Some acquaint-ance with platonic theories is indispensable to every student of modern philosophy.

A Critical History of Modern Aesthetics
Demy 8vo. by the EARL OF LISTOWEL 10s. 6d.

"Lord Listowel gives a careful account of the work done everywhere, and does it with scholarship and selection. . . . Taken as a whole, the book is an excellent and learned guide to the subject, and the author has done a signal service."—*Manchester Guardian*

All prices are net

LONDON : GEORGE ALLEN & UNWIN LTD